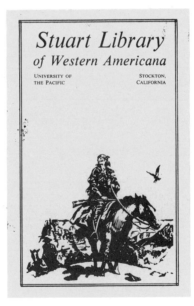

The
Cattle-Trailing
Industry

Jimmy M. Skaggs received his
M.A. and Ph.D. in history from Texas
Tech University, where he served as
Deputy Archivist of the Southwest
Collection. He has published numerous articles on Western American
economic history, is Associate Editor
and Book Review Editor for *Military
History of Texas and the Southwest,*
and is a member of the editorial
board of the *Great Plains Journal.* He
has been assistant professor of economics at Wichita State University
since 1970.

The Cattle

Trailing Industry
Between Supply and Demand, 1866-1890

by
Jimmy M. Skaggs

THE UNIVERSITY PRESS OF KANSAS
Lawrence / Manhattan / Wichita

© Copyright 1973 by The University Press of Kansas
Standard Book Number 7006-0101-5
Library of Congress Catalog Card Number 72-92903
Printed in the United States of America
Designed by John Verburg

Preface

AT SOME unremembered date, while researching my master's thesis on the Western Cattle Trail, I happened upon the exploits of John T. Lytle, who was credited with having driven more than one-half million cattle to market during the last half of the nineteenth century. Intrigued by his alleged activities, which seemed far beyond the ability of one man or firm, I began a casual investigation of his career. I soon discovered an even more fascinating (and equally obscure) example of American entrepreneurial genius—the activities of the cattle-trailing contractors. This study began at that point.

Although a four-year search for the records of any of the major contracting companies has been fruitless, the staffs of many archival repositories have aided greatly in the effort and, in any case, uncovered valuable documents bearing on the subject. The Southwest Collection at Texas Tech University, Lubbock, directed by Professor Roy Sylvan Dunn, was laid open to me in the true tradition of the public-domain manuscript depository. Without the cooperation, understanding, and efforts of Professor Dunn and his staff, this study would have been impossible. Gratitude is also expressed to Eugene D. Decker and Joseph W. Snell, Archivist and Assistant Archivist, respectively, of the Kansas State Historical Society, Topeka; Glen W. Faris, Executive Vice-President, National Cowboy Hall of Fame and Western Heritage Center, Oklahoma City; Dr. Gene M. Gressley, Director of the Western History Research Center at the University of Wyoming, Laramie; Dr. Chester V. Kielman, Archivist of the University of Texas at Austin; Dr. Dorman Winfrey and John M. Kinney, Director and Archivist, respectively, Texas State Library, Austin; Boone McClure, Director of the Panhandle-Plains Historical Museum, Canyon, Texas; Frank Aydelotte and Louis George Griffin, III, past Curator and present Curator, respectively, Regional History Department, University of Kansas; and Michael D. Heaston, Curator of Special Collections, Ablah Library, Wichita State University.

Special appreciation is gratefully offered to the Honorable George Mahon, Representative of the Nineteenth Texas Congressional District, who aided in the location of certain elusive materials in the National Archives; to historian-rancher-critic J. Evetts Haley of Canyon, Texas, who allowed me to leaf through his voluminous, personal research files; to Professor William R. Johnson, Texas Tech, who read and criticized parts of the manuscript; and to Professor James A. Wilson of Southwest Texas State University, who shared his own research findings with me and offered numerous, helpful suggestions.

Being fortunate enough to publish preliminary findings as my research progressed, I would like to thank for their aid editors L. Tuffly Ellis and Joe B. Frantz of the Texas State Historical Association; F. Earl Green of the West Texas Museum Association; Rupert N. Richardson of the West Texas Historical Association; and Steve Wilson of the Institute of the Great Plains. These men have offered much critical comment and graciously allowed me to reuse articles and, more important, ideas which first appeared in their respective journals.

Sincere appreciation is expressed to professors Lowell L. Blaisdell, James V. Reese, David M. Vigness, and Ernest Wallace of the Department of History at Texas Tech and to Dr. Thomas K. Kim, President of McMurry College, formerly Professor of Economics at Texas Tech, each of whom served on my doctoral supervisory committee, read the original draft of this manuscript when it was presented as my dissertation, and contributed to its final form by making perceptive suggestions for improvement.

But no words of gratitude could possibly absolve me of my debt to Professor Seymour V. Connor who encouraged the original idea and directed the dissertation version—all the while reducing my windmills to manageable size; to my close personal friend, Dr. David B. Gracy, II, Archivist of the Southern Labor History Archives, Georgia State University, who read over, argued about, and contributed materially to every finding offered herein; and to my beloved wife, Janette, who typed much of the manuscript and helped with a myriad of other, necessary details. But for whatever may be wrong with the piece, I accept full responsibility. No one else deserves any part of it.

JIMMY M. SKAGGS
Wichita State University

Contents

Illustrations

Hip-Pocket
Businessmen

1

IF THERE IS an American genius, it is the uncanny ability to improvise, to innovate. In post–Civil War Texas, where literally millions of marketable beeves needed only to be driven northward for sale for substantial profits, deft entrepreneurs, many without money enough to buy a single steer (much less an entire trail herd), organized an industry that filled the economic vacuum between supply and demand. The cattle-trailing industry was born.

When a landless cattleman during the immediate postwar era rounded up unbranded and unclaimed maverick cattle, hired drovers with merely the promise of wages after the animals had been sold, begged and borrowed the necessary supplies and equipment, and then set out toward some northern railhead-market, he had no ranch to worry about. He had no need to concern himself with the welfare of calves to be born, with rustlers, or with mortgage payments, for he owned nothing except the animals he claimed. But however popular mavericking might have been, it soon gave way to more practical and standard methods of operation. Livestock were branded, herded, and kept track of by full-time cowhands.[1]

The successful ranching operation—which bought or leased pastures adequate for grazing purposes, stocked its range with cattle, and hired cowboys to oversee the menial but fundamental task of raising them—did not rely upon the whimsical fortunes of fate to supply it with sufficient marketable livestock. It actively engaged in animal husbandry. A rancher could ill-afford

Portions of this chapter appeared in "Hip Pocket Businessmen: The Cattle-Trailing Contractors," *Great Plains Journal*, X (Fall, 1970), 1–10, and are reproduced herein through the courtesy of the Institute of the Great Plains.

to send his employees northward with a trail herd, for the men were needed on the ranch far more than they were needed on the trail. A herd of 3,000 head of cattle required a minimum of eleven drovers, including the trail boss, plus a considerable amount of food, horses, and assorted paraphernalia.[2] Except for the very shortest of drives (one hundred miles or less), most operations, such as the Spur Ranch in Dickens County, Texas, hired professional trail bosses rather than divert experienced ranch employees to gruelling trail drives of several months' duration. Similarly, the Francklyn Land and Cattle Company, located in the Panhandle of Texas, relied primarily on professional contractors to drive its beeves to market.[3]

The huge Matador Land and Cattle Company, a Dundee, Scotland-based corporation, starting in the 1880s in Motley, Dickens, Cottle, and Floyd counties, Texas, even more than its neighbor, the Spur Ranch, recognized the absolute advantages of keeping its cowboys on its own range. It was not uncommon for the Matador to secure the services of a "contractor" who, for a set fee, trailed the ranch's herds to Kansas.[4] After all, as ranch manager H. H. Campbell openly acknowledged, maintaining the ranch was arduous enough without the additional obligation of a trail drive:

> The branding of over 21,000 calves, the gathering and bringing back into the range about 5,000 head of cattle that had drifted off it during the winter months, the separation from the other cattle, and driving into the beef pasture, which first had to be cleared of stock cattle, over 20,000 steers, and the driving to the railroad over 3,000 beeves [had to be done]; after all this work I think it not surprising that our horses became dreadfully poor, that as a consequence, for the past two months, we have not been able to do anything like the same [usual] amount of work . . . .[5]

Cattle-trailing contractors were successful businessmen because it was considerably less expensive to trail livestock to Kansas, where the cattle either were sold to buyers there or shipped to central livestock markets, than to ship direct by rail from Texas. The Missouri, Kansas and Texas and the Texas and Pacific railroads charged $5.00 and $5.50 per head, respectively,

2

from Dallas to St. Louis, while the Santa Fe charged an average of $3.50 from Ellsworth, Kansas, to St. Louis—approximately the same distance. Even after the expense of trailing a herd to Kansas was deducted, it was cheaper to trail, and when dealing with thousands of beeves, the difference of a few dollars per head in transportation expenses was staggering. Many small cattlemen could not afford the initial cost of outfitting a trail drive; others disliked the task of directing drives. For a flat fee, usually $1.00 to $1.50 per head, a trailing contractor furnished the drovers, wagons, supplies, and competent trail bosses and sold the cattle for the rancher on the northern market.[6] Not only did this represent saving of hundreds, even thousands of dollars for Texas ranchers, but as well it relieved them of the burdensome responsibility of the drive.

The contractor's financial successes, in turn, rested upon his efficiency. Ike T. Pryor, a particularly successful transportation agent (a businessman who contracted the delivery of cattle), noted that as late as 1884, a 3,000-head herd could be moved inexpensively: "The salaries of [eleven drovers] . . ., including the boss, were $30.00 each for the ten men, including the cook, and $100.00 a month for the boss. This gave an outlay of $400.00 a month; and estimating $100.00 for provisions, there was an expense of $500.00 a month to move a herd of 3,000 cattle 450 to 500 miles."[7] In less than two months, a 3,000-head herd could be driven from South Texas to a Kansas railhead for a total cost of no more than $1,000. A contractor, receiving from $1.00 to $1.50 per head as his delivery fee, thus stood to clear at least $2,000— less the value of livestock lost en route, which, according to Pryor, seldom exceeded 3 percent, payable at low Texas market prices.[8]

If a concern was efficient, its volume could provide excellent profits. Pryor, in 1884, delivered under contract more than 45,000 cattle to northern ranchers in the Dakotas, Montana, and Wyoming. That distance required three months' travel time, but even so he cleared more than $1,000 on each of fifteen 3,000-head herds, for a total profit of more than $20,000.[9]

The business of cattle-trail contracting attracted a wide variety of opportunistic individuals, many of whom became important men in the cattle industry. D. R. Fant of Goliad, Texas, for an example, drove more than 150,000 head of livestock from Texas to the Indian Territory where they were sold to the gov-

3

ernment; less than one-half were actually owned by him, the remainder having been contracted for delivery and sale from among his neighboring ranchers. George Washington Littlefield, whose name became synonymous with success in the Texas cattle industry, gathered a herd of 1,300 beeves in 1871—600 of which were his own—and drove them to Abilene, Kansas, for sale. Although Littlefield's method included the buying of livestock on credit from other ranchers and therefore was not contracting, per se, the end result was the same. Indeed, his profits were larger than the traditional transportation agent's only because he speculated on market prices.[10]

There were innumerable methods of cattle-trail contracting. There were those who relied entirely upon the capricious trailing business for their livelihood, as D. R. Fant apparently did. Some, such as John T. Lytle of South Texas, essentially were trailing contractors and yet were known on occasion to purchase livestock for speculative purposes. John Henry Stephens of Kyle, Texas, who maintained himself primarily as a Kansas City cattle buyer, often engaged in trail contracting, thereby extracting his profits both from driving the animals to market and from buying slaughter cattle for several St. Louis and Chicago packing houses.[11]

Whatever the precise method of operation, the motive was simply to make a profit. John S. Kritzer of Taylor, Texas, after having returned to the United States from the ill-fated Confederate colony, Carlotta, in Mexico, launched his first drive in 1869. He bought some 7,000 Texas cattle, drove them to Fort Sill, Indian Territory, and sold them to the army. During the next three years, he bought varying numbers of livestock and trailed the cattle to markets outside Texas. In 1874, however, he gathered a large herd of animals from John S. Chisum who, because he was transferring his ranch operations to New Mexico and did not wish to undertake the movement of all his Jinglebob cattle, sold most of his Concho County, Texas, herd cheaply; Kritzer also that year bought livestock from the highly reputable Coggin brothers of Brown County, Texas. Before the drover could market the animals, Texas fever destroyed the whole herd—a capital loss of some $21,000. Thereafter, Kritzer lacked adequate funds to buy the beeves he trailed to market; thus, he became a trailing contractor, supervising the movement of the herds of others. By 1882, he was moving upwards of 10,000 steers a year

4

for North Texas cattle baron Dan Waggoner and was driving other livestock he secured from smaller ranchers—clearing as much as $72,000 in a single season.[12]

Driving Texas cattle northward for sale could be fantastically profitable. George Webb Slaughter, an unusually adroit cattleman and the father of several Southwestern ranchers, found the practice so lucrative that each year, after 1868, he gathered his own marketable steers and, with some or all of his six sons, set out for Kansas, where in eight years he disposed of almost one-half million dollars' worth of livestock:

Year	Number of cattle	Price
1868	800	$32,000.00
1869	2000	90,000.00
1870	2000	105,000.00
1871	unknown	
1872	2000	66,000.00
1873	2000	66,000.00
1874	2000	60,000.00
1775	1000	45,000.00[13]

Had not failing health compelled him to retire, doubtless even more of Slaughter's animals would have been driven to Abilene and Dodge City. But George Webb Slaughter was the exception to the rule. Whereas most of his fellow ranchers either sold their cattle to buyers (who in turn transported the beeves northward and eastward to markets) or relied on the expert services of a trailing contractor, thereby speculating on receiving substantially higher prices for their livestock at the railhead-markets, Slaughter had enough sons to see his cattle safely through to Kansas— without jeopardizing his operations or his herd's welfare.

Perhaps no name is more closely identified with the cattle industry during this period than that of Charles Goodnight, who, not unlike many other Texas cattle barons of the late nineteenth century, began in business essentially as a trailing contractor. In association with Oliver Loving in 1866, Goodnight contracted to supply slaughter animals to the government at Fort Sumner, New Mexico, but Loving was killed by Indians that year, necessitating a new agreement. Then, in 1867, after having established a pasture of his own at Bosque Grande, New Mexico, Goodnight

5

negotiated a pact with John S. Chisum, who at that time still ranched in Concho County, Texas, whereby,

> He [Chisum] was to deliver to me [Goodnight] all the cattle he could handle at Bosque Grande on the Pecos River, I allowing him one dollar per head profit over Texas prices for his risk [in trailing them westward]. During the contract or agreement, he lost two herds by the Indians. I handled the rest of his drives from Bosque Grande west [sic], disposing of them in Colorado and Wyoming. This continued for three years, I dividing the profits equally with him. These profits enabled him to buy the 60,000 head he once held on the Pecos [River] in New Mexico.[14]

Goodnight used his earnings from the enterprise similarly to establish his own ranch on the Arkansas River above Pueblo, Colorado, about 1871.[15]

For the transportation agent, such as Goodnight, his problems were the sum total of the cattle under contract, multiplied by the unforeseen difficulties of the drive. Since rustling was a felonious offense throughout the range cattle region, the trail boss needed either a bill-of-sale for the livestock (if he had purchased them) or a document giving him, in effect, power-of-attorney for the owner. The Coggin brothers of Central Texas insisted on a thorough, legal document whenever they contracted to deliver any cattle:

> State of Texas
> County of Brown
> Known [sic] all men by these present that I, Rob-[er]t Trogdon [?] of the County of Brown and State of Texas: have this day, Authorized Samuel and M. J. Coggin of the County of Coleman and State aforesaid to gether [sic], drive, sell and deliver any Cattle found on the Range or Hurd [sic] or in possession of parties not my agents: in the following Mark and Brand Here in after [sic] mentioned to witt [sic].[16]

Then followed a four-column, two-page list of earmarks and brands to which the rancher held legal title.

But what, for example, if in the course of a drive an agent

6

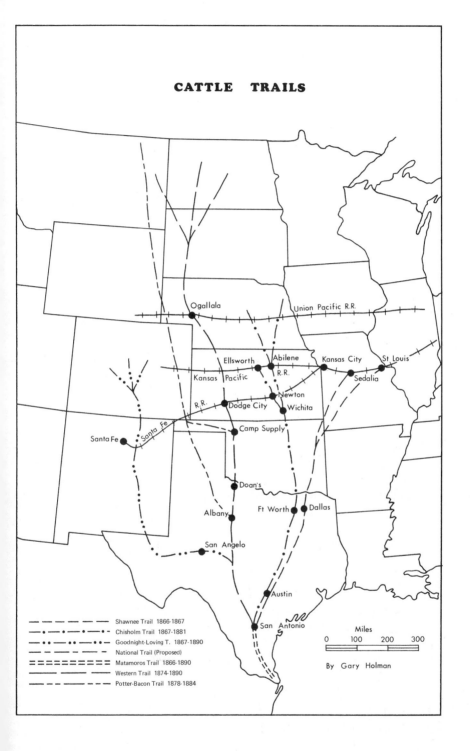

CATTLE TRAILS

Ogallala

Union Pacific R.R.

Ellsworth · Abilene · Kansas City · St Louis

Kansas Pacific · R.R. · Sedalia

R.R. · Dodge City · Newton · Wichita

Santa Fe · Santa Fe · Camp Supply

Doan's

Albany · Ft Worth · Dallas

San Angelo

Austin

San Antonio

Miles
0   100   200   300

By Gary Holman

Shawnee Trail 1866-1867
Chisholm Trail 1867-1881
Goodnight-Loving T. 1867-1890
National Trail (Proposed)
Matamoros Trail 1866-1890
Western Trail 1874-1890
Potter-Bacon Trail 1878-1884

Oliver Loving, a pioneering contractor, blazed a cattle trailing to New Mexico in association with Charles Goodnight. Loving, while driving cattle over the route he opened, was killed by Indians in 1866. *Photo courtesy of the Museum and the Southwest Collection, Texas Tech University.*

Charles Armand Schreiner, a Texas merchant, was a partner in the Lytle, McDaniel, Schreiner, and Light Cattle Company, a firm which trailed more cattle to the northern railhead-markets than any other transportation agency. *Photo courtesy of the Museum and the Southwest Collection, Texas Tech University.*

John R. Blocker, co-owner of the Blocker Brothers and Jennings Cattle Company, drove cattle northward as late as the 1890s. His firm was one of the three largest of all the transportation agencies. *Photo courtesy of the Museum and the Southwest Collection, Texas Tech University.*

John T. Lytle, founder of the Lytle, McDaniel, Schreiner, and Light Cattle Company, directed the movement of more range and ranch cattle than any other transportation agent. *Photo courtesy of the Museum and the Southwest Collection, Texas Tech University.*

Dillard Rucker Fant began driving livestock northward for sale in 1869. By 1885, when he contracted the delivery of his last herd of cattle, Fant was responsible for the movement of almost 200,000 beeves. *Photo courtesy of the Museum and the Southwest Collection, Texas Tech University.*

William Henry Jennings went to work in 1874 as a cattle buyer for the Blocker Brothers Cattle Company. Six years later he became a full partner in the operation. He later diversified by becoming a rancher. *Photo courtesy of the Museum and the Southwest Collection, Texas Tech University.*

George Washington Littlefield returned to Texas from the Civil War and began transporting cattle to northern markets. His profits eventually enabled him to become one of the state's most successful ranchers and bankers. *Photo courtesy of the Museum and the Southwest Collection, Texas Tech University.*

George W. Saunders became a drover while still a teenager. Within a decade he owned his own trailing firm, driving both horses and cattle northward for sale. He later helped to organize the Union Stock Yards Company at San Antonio. *Photo courtesy of the Museum and the Southwest Collection, Texas Tech University.*

Able Head (Shanghai) Pierce, a substantial Texas rancher, occasionally supplemented his income by contracting the delivery of cattle to northern markets. *Photo courtesy of the Western History Collections, University of Oklahoma Library.*

Martin S. Culver (c. 1880), who later became a prominent Texas rancher, during the 1870s served as overseer for the Lytle, McDaniel, Schreiner, and Light Cattle Company. *Photo courtesy of the Western History Collections, University of Oklahoma Library.*

Charles Goodnight, a major figure in the Texas ranching industry, helped to blaze the Goodnight-Loving Trail to New Mexico and contracted the delivery of livestock over that path during the 1860s and 1870s. *Photo courtesy of the Western History Collections, University of Oklahoma Library.*

L. B. Anderson, who later reminisced in *The Trail Drivers of Texas*, bossed drives for several transportation agencies, such as the Lytle, McDaniel, Schreiner, and Light and the Ellison and Dewees cattle companies. *Photo courtesy of the Western History Collections, University of Oklahoma Library.*

discovered that somehow he had acquired beeves that he had no legal right to drive or sell? When a reputable contractor found he inadvertently had gathered stray beeves along the way, he made restitution, or, when he deposited the money from the sale of cattle for his client, he advised the rancher of the situation. It was then the responsibility of the rancher, who had hired the transportation agent, to make restitution for the illegal sale of cattle. S. W. Lomax of the Spur Ranch, for example, wrote a neighbor:

> It has just come to our attention that in a herd of ours shipped to the Berry Cattle Co[mpany] of Montana, was a steer branded LG on the side, and I lose no time in acquainting you with the fact, and beg to enclose in settlement for same our cheque for thirteen dollars. Our steers sold for $13.50 and the expense against the drive was 50¢ per head, leaving $13.00 nett [sic].
>
> Please sign and return the enclosed receipt.[17]

Or, as Lomax once advised Mrs. S. A. Camel of Abilene, Texas, regarding the unauthorized sale of ninety-six of her animals that had been mistakenly gathered by Spur hands and driven to market by the contractor:

40 head in herd No. 1 at $21.50	$860.00
46 head in herd No. 2	
−3 head lost	
43 head sold at $17.00	731.00
Total sales	$1591.00
less amount charged by [trailing] co[mpany] for driving same	83.00
Nett [sic] proceeds	$1508.00[18]

But not all trailing operations were perfectly reputable. One drive in 1876 to the Black Hills of the Dakotas, under the command of Joel Collins, ended unsatisfactorily for the owner of the livestock, for Collins and a youthful accomplice, Sam Bass, gambled and drank away the proceeds from the cattle sale. Thus began their lives of crime.[19]

Collins and Bass, however, were atypical of drovers and of the crimes usually associated with transportation agencies. To

7

reduce their own shrinkage, some trail bosses appropriated cattle that had strayed from nearby ranches or previous trail herds and butchered them, thereby furnishing fresh meat for their drovers. Zack Stucker, employed by John T. Lytle in the early 1870s as a trail boss, frequently rustled steers along the trail. Even when a trail boss steadfastly opposed such practices, his drovers might occasionally slaughter a stray animal—totally without his knowledge. Jim Wilson, a drover for Eugene B. Millett of South Texas, for an example, admitted that he and the cook once butchered an animal lost from a previous Lytle herd without the trail boss ever learning of their crime.[20]

Too, there was the problem of transit through the Indian Territory. Almost from the outset of commercial trailing in 1866, bands of Indians had demanded and usually received cattle from trail herds in payment for allowing the Texans to cross their reserves unmolested. For an example, Quanah Parker, a Comanche war chief, in the late 1870s and early 1880s stationed himself in the Wichita Mountains near Fort Sill and exacted tribute from each trail herd he encountered. Consequently, trail bosses not infrequently bought the friendly relations of Indians with stray cattle they had gathered along the way. On one occasion, William Jackman, a minor South Texas contractor who trail bossed his own herds to Kansas, happened upon a steer owned by Ike Pryor and lost on a previous drive. Jackman, planning to deliver the animal to Pryor at Dodge City, included it in his herd and moved on. Near Fort Sill, the drive was stopped by a band of forty Indians who handed the Texan a scrawled note which read:

> To the trail bosses:
> This man is a good Indian; I know him personally. Treat him well, give him a beef, and you will have no trouble in driving through this country.
>> (Signed)
>> Ike T. Pryor

Jackman immediately ordered Pryor's steer cut out of the herd and dutifully delivered it to the Indians.[21]

The substantial contractor who, unlike Jackman, remained behind in Texas to oversee his entire operation, knew little and probably cared less about the minor illicit activities of his employees. Other matters demanded his attention. John Henry

Stephens agonized over the hiring of trail bosses for herds under his control, because a competent leader often meant the difference between profits and losses. Similarly, the precise path a given herd was to follow was a matter of major significance. The overall direction was easily determined, for a herd was driven over a given trail to a specific point. Nevertheless, because of drought conditions, previously heavy trail traffic, or any number of other reasons, a herd might deviate several miles from the route of a certain cattle trail. If several thousand head of cattle were under contract from one ranch, as in the case of an 1885 Stephens agreement, numerous herds might be sent along a parallel course so that the later bunches would not suffer from an overgrazed trail left by those that had gone before. And, when dealing with a large, foreign-owned corporation, such as the Matador Ranch, Stephens needed to account for every head of livestock, lest his reliability as a contractor be challenged and reputation damaged.[22]

When contracts were negotiated on a cost-plus basis, i.e., where the ranch paid all expenses of the drive plus a set fee for the contractor, the maintenance of meticulously accurate records was of paramount importance. Most contractors desired or kept few records. This laxity could cause major problems for the rancher involved in a cost-plus agreement. William Sommerville advised his superior in Dundee, Scotland,

> It is a matter of considerable difficulty to obtain vouchers for everything paid out on the trail; we made our instructions before hand as plain as possible; but we could see it was next to impossible to get accurate vouchers for everything. Payment [of salaries] are sometimes made to the men under circumstances when the obtaining of vouchers is impracticable. The store accounts against [John H.] Stephens and [John T.] Lytle at different stopping places were so mixed up with personal accounts and cash drawings by the several outfits [several herds], that the obtaining of accurate vouchers for each individual outfit would have required the strenuous efforts of some one man, whose attention would have had to be entirely occupied with it.[23]

Nothwithstanding the obvious problems relative to these

9

arrangements, they were most advantageous for the cattlemen. As Sommerville once explained to the careful Scots, even though the Matador Ranch had decided to go to the additional trouble and expense of sending one of its own, trusted employees out ahead of the drive—to make certain the route selected was well watered and had sufficient grass for the cattle—the agreement with the trailing company was considered in the best interests of the ranch, for "we shall get our cattle to market at about half the present cost."[24] The gigantic XIT Ranch similarly saw the profitable advantages of using these transportation agents; in 1889, even after the decline of cattle trailing, it continued to shun local railroad service by hiring professional drovers to move six herds to leased pastures in Montana, reportedly saving the Capitol Freehold Land and Investment Company (corporate name of the XIT) some $60,000.[25]

The significance of the trailing contractor both as a transporter of livestock and as a cattleman during the period is obvious. Research, even by those not especially interested in the contractor, points up that these businessmen played a major role in the range cattle industry. Writer Wayne Gard found that in 1875, four transportation agents (Eugene B. Millett, Seth Mabry, John O. Dewees, and James F. Ellison) owned or controlled an estimated two-thirds of the 150,000 cattle driven from Texas that year.[26] And although doubtlessly accurate, Gard's information was incomplete. The activities of at least a half-dozen other contracting concerns could have been added to that total to have pushed the percentage even higher.

Even though the role of the cattle-trailing contractor between 1866 and 1890 was of major significance, it is doubtful that a precisely accurate assessment of the total number of livestock handled by them will ever be obtained. The firm of Lytle, McDaniel, Schreiner, and Light—probably the largest of all such operations—apparently kept few office files, if any.[27] Indeed, few records were needed. One letter could cover an agreement between rancher and contractor for the movement of 25,000 cattle,[28] and a single legal document could authorize the transportation and sale of several herds of livestock.[29] Because of this method of operation, which might best be described as a hip-pocket business, there is a definite inadequacy of documentation in the form of primary business records. The records available are

10

merely those that were maintained by the rancher; thus, but a fragment of the overall story has been preserved.

Available sources—contemporary newspaper accounts,[30] published and unpublished reminiscences, and related ranch records—clearly demonstrate that the role of the cattle-trailing contractor, as a Texas businessman and as a transporter of livestock, was more than merely significant. The 1875 figures, in which four agents controlled the movement of no less than two-thirds of all the animals trailed northward from Texas for sale, are but one of many examples that could be cited.

The Trail Drivers of Texas, compiled and edited by J. Marvin Hunter under the supervision of the Trail Drivers Association of Texas, and released in its most complete edition in 1925, is probably the best, single source for the drovers' memoirs and, incidentally, for the activities of transportation agents. Since these entrepreneurs hired the majority of the men who drove cattle, and since these workers later reminisced freely in this volume, the bosses discussed most frequently were the very cattlemen who handled the greatest volume of livestock—the trailing contractors. Containing more than three hundred separate accounts of the movement of Longhorns, this work clearly shows that substantially more than half of the beeves driven to market in any given year were moved by people other than the ranchers who had raised the animals.[31]

Numerous and diverse Texans were engaged in the various aspects of this enterprise. The examples of Charles Goodnight, John S. Chisum, and George W. Littlefield already have been given, but these were not the men who became leaders in contracting cattle to northern railheads and ranges. Although literally hundreds of people at one time or another apparently tried a hand at the business,[32] available sources indicate that no more than a handful of men achieved any degree of prominence. Lytle, McDaniel, Schreiner, and Light; Eugene B. Millett and associates; the Blocker brothers; the Pryor brothers; Monroe Choate and associates; J. F. Ellison and John O. Dewees; J. J. Myres; George W. Saunders, and a few others were the major companies and individuals involved. Since they were responsible for the movement of most of the cattle that left Texas for northern ranges and markets between 1866 and 1890, the story is largely theirs.

11

Lytle, McDaniel, Schreiner, and Light: 2
Entrepreneurs

THE TERM "cattle baron" invariably is used in reference to ranchers who amassed large landed estates, and countless cattlemen—such as Richard King of the King Ranch, Samuel Burk Burnett of the 6666 Ranch, George W. Littlefield of the LFD Ranch, and Charles Goodnight of the JA Ranch—could be included within that classification. Yet there were many nineteenth-century cattle barons who built considerable personal fortunes without acquiring huge tracts of land or by subordinating land acquisition to other lucrative aspects of the open-range cattle industry. John T. Lytle, Thomas M. McDaniel, Charles Schreiner, and John W. Light were such entrepreneurs who, through their control of the largest of all the cattle-trailing companies, came to symbolize success in the transportation phase of the Texas cattle industry during the last three decades of the nineteenth century —and who, by making millions in the process, were cattle barons in their own right.

John Thomas Lytle, the organizing genius behind the Lytle, McDaniel, Schreiner, and Light Cattle Company, was born on October 8, 1844, at McSherrystown, Adams County, Pennsylvania. His parents, Francis and Margaret (Collins) Lytle, along with his uncle, William Lytle, had migrated in the early 1830s from southern Ireland to Pennsylvania where Francis was employed as a teacher. William soon moved on to join friends in Maryland, and a few years later he migrated westward to Texas. In 1860, at William's encouragement, Francis moved his family

Portions of this chapter appeared in "John Thomas Lytle: Cattle Baron," *Southwestern Historical Quarterly*, LXXI (July, 1967), 46–60, and are reproduced herein through the courtesy of the Texas State Historical Association.

of eight, in which John was the third child and the only son, to William's Atascosa County ranch. Not long thereafter, the newcomers relocated at San Antonio where Francis obtained a teaching position. Sixteen-year-old John readily went to work in the Bexar County clerk's office, but after a year, poor health compelled him to resign.[1]

To regain his health and perhaps to relieve a manpower shortage caused by the Civil War, he accepted his uncle's offer of work on the ranch. For $15 a month, he worked from dawn to dusk, simultaneously, albeit slowly, regaining his health and developing his ability as a cowboy. In 1862, possibly because of the continuing labor shortage, but probably because he was the boss's nephew, he was named foreman. The war, however, was far more exciting, and the young foreman soon decided to abandon the humdrum of ranching for the supposed glamour of musketry and battle.[2]

Unfortunately, only a fragment of Lytle's participation in the conflict is known. One writer[3] states that Lytle held a commission during the war; confirmation of this, however, has not been found. Whatever his rank, after the war he was almost invariably known as Captain Lytle.[4] Available information gives merely a brief outline of his service. After he enlisted on September 11, 1863, in San Antonio, he joined Company H, Thirty-second Texas Cavalry (Wood's Regiment), at Fort Clark, near Brackettville, Texas. Except for the brief period from February 2 to June 1, 1864, when he and his cousin Samuel Lytle, commander of Company H, were on detached service in pursuit of deserters, John remained at the fort, rising to the rank of sergeant, apparently without once having seen battle. He was paroled on August 29, 1865, at San Antonio and allowed to return home.[5]

For the next two years, while Lytle again worked on his uncle William's ranch, he was thoroughly impressed by the rapidly widening business opportunities of the cattle trade. By 1867, Texas cattlemen had begun to exploit the fabulous profits to be made by trailing their livestock to eager purchasers at northern railheads. The North, rapidly industrializing in the wake of the Civil War and with a scarcity of some foods, such as beef, because of inroads resulting from the recent conflict, bid up the price of cattle; moreover, the army faced the task of feeding troops and conquered Indian tribes. Consequently, Texas Long-

14

horns—although producing beef that was tough and stringy, yet comparatively palatable—commanded from $18 to $50 each at the railhead-markets. In 1866, Texans had driven more than a quarter-million head to Sedalia, Missouri, then the closest railhead. Seeing a fortune awaiting him, in January, 1867, Lytle resigned as foreman of his uncle's ranch, and, apparently with borrowed money, he leased a small pasture near Castroville, Texas, on the Medina River, stocked it with 1,500 Longhorns, and became a rancher.[6]

While ranching in Medina County, he met and in 1867 married Elizabeth Noonan, a member of a prominent Medina County ranching family and a sister of influential Judge George Henry Noonan, who later (1895–1897) served the San Antonio region in the Fifty-fourth Congress. The Lytles had two children, a boy, George, and a girl, Helen. A third child was stillborn in 1875, and Elizabeth died of complications shortly thereafter.[7]

After Elizabeth's death, and possibly because of it, Lytle plunged with all his energy into his already extensive cattle business. In 1871, he had formed a partnership in what is now Lytle, Texas, with Thomas M. McDaniel, whose daughter, Sarah, had married Charles Lytle, William's oldest son.[8] Unfortunately, little is known of McDaniel's background or previous business activity.

In addition to trailing their own herds to northern railheads and ranges, Lytle and McDaniel contracted to furnish hands and equipment for other ranchers, and soon this service became the mainstay of the Lytle and McDaniel Cattle Company. Indeed, the business grew so rapidly that by 1874 additional capitalization was needed to serve adequately a large and constantly expanding list of clients. Consequently, that year they sold to Charles Schreiner and John W. Light one-half interest in the concern.[9]

Charles Armand Schreiner, a Kerrville, Texas, merchant, is an excellent example of frontier business diversification and acumen. Schreiner, the son of Dr. Gustave Adolph and Charlotte (Bippert) Schreiner, was born on February 22, 1938, in the Alsatian community of Riguewihr, France. In 1852, along with his parents, two brothers, and two sisters, he migrated to the United States, taking up residence in San Antonio. Shortly thereafter, Charles's father died; four years later his mother was buried

15

near San Antonio, and Charles, eighteen years of age, joined the Texas Rangers, with which he remained for three years. In 1857, tired of his demanding frontier-service assignment in the rocky region that lies along the Rio Grande between the Devils and Pecos rivers, he joined with his brother-in-law, Caspar Real, in a ranching enterprise along the Turtle Creek tributary of the Guadalupe River in Kerr County, Texas. Thereafter, only service in the War of the Rebellion with the Third Texas Infantry, from 1861 to 1865, interrupted Schreiner's concerted effort to become a successful businessman.[10]

In 1869, Schreiner persuaded August Faltin, a Comfort, Texas, merchant, to furnish $5,000 worth of financial backing for a mercantile establishment in the frontier village of Kerrville, Texas. Schreiner ran the operation, he and Faltin sharing equally in the profits. The first year the store grossed more than $5,000, and in 1879 Schreiner purchased Faltin's share of the operation. There appears little doubt that Schreiner's investment in and profits from the Lytle, McDaniel, Schreiner, and Light Cattle Company, after 1874, contributed substantially to his financial independence from Faltin.[11]

John W. Light, not unlike his fellow Hill Country resident, Charles Schreiner, was also adept at making money. The son of Hiram and Elizabeth (Henion) Light, John W. Light was born on July 16, 1844, in Putman County, New York. In 1861, then seventeen years of age, he enlisted with the Sixth New York Heavy Artillery, serving in the Wilderness Campaign and rising to the rank of sergeant by the end of the war. Following his release from active duty in 1865, Light migrated westward to Leavenworth, Kansas, where he soon found employment as a teamster with a wagon train en route to Santa Fe. In 1867, he obtained a contract to supply Kansas military posts with slaughter animals. Although the business was profitable, poor investments left him totally ruined by 1872 when he left for Texas "to begin life anew."[12] Light was soon hired as a laborer by Ben Gooch, a Mason County stock raiser, and, the following year, he bought out his employer, signing a three-year promissory note for $18,000. In 1874, with 2,500 head of his own livestock as the nucleus of a trail herd and with financial backing from Seth Mabry, an Austin, Texas, cattle-trailing contractor, Light gathered some 5,000 cattle, drove them to Ogallala, Nebraska, and

16

sold them for a "substantial profit." Light apparently invested his new-found capital in the Lytle, McDaniel, Schreiner, and Light Cattle Company, and, before the end of the decade, his net worth was estimated to be well in excess of $100,000.[13]

The Lytle, McDaniel, Schreiner, and Light Company's method of operation was disarmingly simple and yet highly efficient. Lytle and McDaniel's base in Lytle, Texas, and Schreiner's store at Kerrville served as staging points for drives. Lytle and Light, with their extensive knowledge of the cattle trade, selected bosses and hired hands for the drives that usually followed the route of the Western Cattle Trail to Dodge City, Kansas. Once herds were on the move, Lytle then proceeded to the northern railheads where he received the livestock and negotiated the sales. McDaniel, Schreiner, and Light usually remained in Texas to supervise operations there and to solicit additional beeves to be trailed. This technique enabled the concern to handle as many as 91,000 head in a single season. On one occasion, in 1885, the company contracted to drive 25,000 head of cattle for the Francklyn Land and Cattle Company, a feat far beyond the ability of most transportation agencies.[14]

Simplicity of organization, however, did not alleviate one major problem faced by all trailing concerns during the early 1870s—the menace of Indian attack. For the first ten years after the Civil War, trail herds en route to Kansas railhead-markets plied the Chisholm Trail through east-central Texas and the more civilized areas of the Indian Territory. But as the farm population of Texas increased and as rail facilities became more readily available in central and western Kansas, contractors began blazing routes farther west. Indeed, Lytle was intrigued by the possibility of a new trail, far west of the Texas frontier, on which his cattle would encounter sufficient pasturage, a virtually treeless topography, and no farmers irate over trampled fields. In 1872, the army—in answer to repeated appeals from Texans in general and cattlemen in particular—ordered Colonel Ranald S. Mackenzie, commanding the Fourth Cavalry at Fort Richardson, Texas, to prevent Indian depredations and to provide trail herds with suitable escorts. Undoubtedly aware of those instructions, Lytle in April, 1874, bossed a 3,000-head herd northwestward from San Antonio to Fort Griffin, Texas, then Mackenzie's headquarters, where he requested an escort through the dangerous

17

Indian Territory to the north. The colonel's command, under-staffed because most of the unit was in the field chasing elusive Kiowas and Comanches, could furnish merely a civilian scout, but Lytle persisted and drove his herd on to Dodge City, thereby blazing the Western Cattle Trail.[15]

Few contractors were willing that year to follow Lytle's dangerous new path, for most drovers preferred farmers to Indians. Fortunately for the transportation agencies, however, the army launched a major campaign before the end of the year to clear the plains of Texas of hostile Indian bands. Late in the fall, Mackenzie's Fourth Cavalry rode northward onto the *Llano Estacado* while Colonel Nelson A. Miles, commanding the Fifth Infantry at Fort Dodge, Kansas, marched southward into the Texas Panhandle. The pincers movement trapped the Indians, and by midsummer, 1875, the Kiowas and Comanches had been completely defeated and placed on a reservation under the watchful eye of the military.[16] Transportation agents, such as Lytle, McDaniel, Schreiner, and Light, were elated.

Soon, the road brands—symbolic of the company's growth and stature—used by Lytle, McDaniel, Schreiner, and Light were fixtures on the new route and became known throughout the cattle kingdom. The L-M brand, originally used by Lytle and McDaniel, was retained and employed by the expanded firm; the S-L mark stood for Schreiner and Lytle; but perhaps the best known identification was the primary road brand, the S L ⅃.[17]

Too, the organization on occasion associated itself with other trail-contracting companies. John Henry Stephens of Kyle, Texas, whose activities as a Kansas City cattle buyer were mentioned earlier, not infrequently joined in temporary albeit profitable partnerships with Lytle's agency, as did Major A. Conkle, a Kansas City promoter and cattle buyer.[18]

The precise number of cattle that Lytle, McDaniel, Schreiner, and Light—as a firm and in association with other agencies—handled over the years probably will never be known, for whatever scant business records the company maintained were either lost or destroyed soon after Lytle's death.[19] Yet, several estimates are credible. The organization between 1871 and 1887 apparently directed the movement of no less than 600,000 head of livestock. Lytle at the turn of the century recalled the yearly figures thus (the 1876 total includes all drives through that year):

18

1876	6,000
1877	15,000
1878	22,000
1879	25,000
1880	40,000
1881	50,000
1882	50,000
1883	70,000
1884	91,000
1885	40,000
1886	25,000
1887	12,000

450,000[20]

Another source indicates that an additional 150,000 head, for some inexplicable reason not counted by Lytle, were moved under the S-L mark. In 1874, the concern reportedly trailed between 1,800 and 2,500 livestock to Kansas railheads. Five years later, positive evidence of the firm's growth—and particularly of Lytle's importance in the company's operation—can be seen. Of the forty-one trail herds (98,510 head) that had passed Fort Griffin, Texas, as of May 29, 1879, en route to Dodge City, Lytle's personal brand (the 7D) was on five (10,350 head), and his organization controlled another herd of 2,300 head, an impressive 13 percent of all the range and ranch cattle traffic that year.[21]

Inasmuch as Lytle did most of his company's hiring and firing, his reputation as an employer is of some significance. Frank Collinson, who went to work for Lytle and McDaniel in December, 1873, to help drive a herd to Fort Robinson, Nebraska, said that Lytle was a good boss but charged that he was generally unconcerned with the overall welfare of his hands. Collinson claimed that Lytle so restricted the amount of personal goods a drover could take with him on a drive that the bedding was skimpy; in fact, the men had to sleep in pairs in order to keep warm. Nevertheless, following the drive, all but four of Lytle's employees eagerly returned to South Texas and happily drove another herd for him. Joe Benton, who worked for Lytle's company in the early 1870s, expressed no grievance against the captain; neither did Oscar Thompson nor Sam Neill, nor any of the others who later recorded their experiences. And one of Lytle's

19

employees, Gus Black, so idolized his boss that he named his son after him. Although Lytle apparently enjoyed the close contact with his men, afforded when he personally bossed herds to northern markets, he soon became too involved in administrative matters and therefore was forced in the latter 1870s to hire many professional trail bosses.[22] He could secure the services of the best men in the business, Harry Sinclair Drago says, because "No wagon ever left Doan's store [ford of the Red River on the Western Trail] until the contents had been checked and rechecked."[23] Corwin Doan, postmaster at Doan's, once observed that Lytle was most careful in regard to the welfare of his men: "Captain Lytle spent as high as a month at a time in Doan's preparing for his onward march. Accompanied by his secretary he would fit out his men, and everything would be shipshape when he crossed the Red River. He was a great man, and his visits were enjoyed."[24]

Contrary to Collinson's opinion, this little extra care and concern for its employees, Drago concludes, resulted in the best cooks, the best riders, and the best bosses competing for jobs with Lytle's organization.[25] Also, as Gus Black, one of the firm's many trail bosses in the later 1870s, pointed out, "Captain Lytle's check was good anywhere in the world," and his word was as good as his check.[26] Although Black was obviously impressed by Lytle—as evidenced by the name Black gave his son—his statement does indicate that Lytle's employees respected him both as an employer and as a man.

Lytle's stature in the cattle industry, i.e., the esteem he was accorded by both his employees and by other cattlemen, is perhaps illustrative of the success of his concern and is probably best seen in the single mention of his name by Andy Adams in *Reed Anthony*. Adams, whose fiction often had the ring of truth because his stories were based on his personal experiences, used Lytle's name, along with others of his stature, to show the humor of drovers. He created a situation whereby cowboys from Texas met in 1881 at Dodge City to organize a social club. Using an official-sounding name, The Juan-Jinglero Company, Ltd., the drovers had stationery printed which showed the concern to be capitalized at $5,000,000 with "John T. Lytle as treasurer, R. G. Head as secretary, Jesse Presnall as Attorney, Captain E. B. Millett as fiscal agent for placing the stock, and a dozen leading drovers as vice presidents." Intended as a joke, according to the novel, soon major companies were fooled by the prominence of its officers and besieged it for information on cattle prices and deliveries.[27] Adams knew Lytle personally, and although the story in *Reed Anthony* probably is fictional, Adams selected the names of outstanding cattlemen, many of whom were transportation agents, to make it realistic. It does not seem coincidental that Lytle's name was listed first, for the book is dedicated

To

CAPTAIN JOHN T. LYTLE

SECRETARY OF

THE TEXAS CATTLE RAISERS' ASSOCIATION

FORT WORTH, TEXAS[28]

In the same way that prominence often connotes success, success in business usually implies shrewdness. To be certain, Lytle and his associates were shrewd businessmen, seldom missing any opportunity that held out the prospect of profit. When in 1875 it was announced that Colonel Ranald S. Mackenzie, commanding at Fort Sill, was to auction off approximately 7,500 Indian ponies surrendered to him by defeated Kiowa and Comanche bands, Lytle went to the reservation to investigate. Although the animals were reportedly in poor condition, he must have believed the low price of $4.00 per head made up for the deficit in quality, for he purchased about one hundred horses, enough for one drive.[29]

Shrewd dealing, however, could also result in a capital loss. Once, when Lytle, McDaniel, Schreiner, and Light associated themselves with Kansas City cattle buyer A. Conkle, the Missourian saw what he thought was an excellent opportunity to save the temporary alliance a large sum of money. Several herds of contracted beeves had been driven through Dodge City by the enlarged firm, and a company employee, Martin Culver, was left at that place to offer rewards ($1.00 per head for steers and $2.00 for horses) for those that had been lost on the trail by the transportation company and that were surrendered to Culver at Dodge City. Ben Hodges, a confidence man of mixed (Negro and Mexican) ancestry, soon obtained some blank receipts, forged them, and entrained for Missouri. When, upon his arrival at Kansas City, Hodges presented the vouchers to Conkle, Lytle's associate decided to drive a hard bargain with this "poor and

21

ignorant Negro cowboy" and redeemed several hundred dollars' worth of bogus receipts by paying Hodges's room and board, providing him with a complete wardrobe, and giving him $60 in cash. Not long thereafter Hodges disappeared, and a chagrined Conkle discovered he had been swindled.[30]

Notwithstanding confidence men such as Hodges, Lytle's firm continued a profitable operation until Texas fever, carried northward by Texas herds, destroyed the business. The disease, a problem that caused Lytle, McDaniel, Schreiner, and Light considerable difficulty, was first detected about 1814, but it was much later, about 1890, that it was conclusively found to be carried by parasitic ticks indigenous to Southwest Texas. Immune Texas cattle transported the malady northward where livestock, once bitten by the ticks, sickened and died. As a result, by 1885, several northern states and territories had legislated quarantines against disease-carrying Texas cattle. And contemporaneous with the quarantines was a decline in the demand for Texas cattle. The Longhorn had long been inferior in quality to beefier northern short-horned livestock, and, by 1885, an increasing supply of improved cattle reduced the demand for trail stock. Texas cattlemen suffered accordingly.[31]

This change in the ratio between supply and demand is easily seen in the example of one of the Lytle, McDaniel, Schreiner, and Light contracts. In early February, 1885, Colonel B. B. Groom, general manager of the Francklyn Land and Cattle Company, contacted Lytle and asked that the captain aid in the marketing of the Francklyn cattle. Organized in 1882 on vast Texas Panhandle-Plains holdings, the Francklyn Company was deeply in debt by 1885 and needed desperately to sell most of its available livestock to meet pressing financial commitments. Colonel Groom confided to Frank G. Brown, the company's secretary in New York, that he planned to hire Lytle and John Henry Stephens[32] to transport and to sell the ranch cattle, for they were "better acquainted with the trade in cattle than any other two men in the country."[33] Toward the end of February, Groom, Lytle, and Stephens agreed that for $1.00 per head, Lytle and Stephens would take charge of all Francklyn livestock in Greer County, see to all matters of the trail, sell the cattle on the northern market, and deposit the proceeds—less their fee—at the direction of the Francklyn Company. Groom was confident of

22

Corwin F. Doan, co-owner of Doan Store on the Western Trail, in *The Trail Drivers of Texas* described many of the transportation agents to whom his firm sold supplies. *Photo courtesy of the Western History Collections, University of Oklahoma Library.*

Huge clouds of dust, stirred up by animals' hooves, was a fact of life on the cattle trail, as in this unidentified scene. *Photo courtesy of the Museum of the Great Plains, Lawton, Oklahoma.*

Branding cattle for the trail frequently required
all hands. Once roped—and not necessarily
about the neck—the animal had to be man-

handled, thrown, and held down while it was
branded. *Photos courtesy of the Museum of
the Great Plains, Lawton, Oklahoma.*

Livestock pens and empty cattle car awaiting the shipment of cattle to market. *Photo courtesy of the Museum of the Great Plains, Lawton, Oklahoma.*

Doan's Store (c. 1889), near the crossing of the Red River, was a favorite supply depot for trail herds using the Western Cattle Trail. *Photo courtesy of the Western History Collections, University of Oklahoma Library.*

Moments of relaxation, while on the trail, usually were reserved for mealtime beside the chuck wagon, as in this scene somewhere on the Plains during the 1880s. *Photo courtesy of the Museum of the Great Plains, Lawton, Oklahoma.*

success, and he wrote to Brown that Lytle and Stephens had "sold between them 75,000 head last year."[34] He therefore believed they would have little difficulty with only one-third that number. Upon the herd's arrival in Cheyenne, Wyoming, in June, Lytle notified Groom that he expected sales to total $100,000 by July 1, $200,000 by August 1, and the balance by mid-September, and that Stephens would be in the Northwest late in the month to aid in the marketing. But on August 26, Lytle wired that he still had 10,700 head of cattle on hand and that the market was closed for the year. He advised Groom that since everyone seemed prone to purchase northern livestock and to wait and see the full impact of the quarantines, Groom should come to Cheyenne and direct the disposal of the cattle. Groom did, and he and Lytle covered the countryside looking for buyers, finally selling the animals at "ruinously low prices." Primarily because of the soft market in 1885, the Francklyn Company was forced into receivership the following year.[35]

With a waning demand in the North for Texas cattle, the firm of Lytle, McDaniel, Schreiner, and Light collapsed. Each year, after 1884, as fewer and fewer cattlemen put their herds on the trail for the North, using Texas railroad facilities instead—even though Texas railroads had not substantially reduced their rates—the need for the company's peculiar service declined. From a high of 91,000 head trailed northward in 1884, the company's volume decreased to 40,000 in 1885, to 25,000 in 1886, and finally to 12,000 in 1887; the enterprise simply could not show a profit with such restricted operations. Similarly, there was relatively little money to be made by buying a herd and delivering it to a railhead a few miles distant. By the spring of 1887, the firm's operation was in such a shaky financial condition that Lytle, McDaniel, and Light agreed to surrender their share of the organization to Schreiner, with the understanding that the Kerrville merchant would assume the accrued indebtedness.[36]

The whole cattle-raising industry, as well as its transportation phase, was undergoing more than a mere cyclical recession; the open range was being fenced, and the trailing of livestock was approaching its end. Such a fundamental alteration of the structure and stability of the cattle trade, especially in Texas, could not help but leave its mark on those who, but a short time before, had profited extensively from the cattle-trailing industry.

Some were destroyed financially. Others shrewdly turned adversity into gain.

If the Lytle, McDaniel, Schreiner, and Light Cattle Company's situation can be considered typical, then it may be inferred that one-half of those businessmen involved in the cattle-trailing industry were wiped out by this transition. John W. Light was so broken by the sale of his share of the company to Schreiner that he was unable to finance his James River Ranch any longer, and he sold the spread to Schreiner. Light then accepted a position on what had been his ranch. For seven years the erstwhile cattle baron managed the merchant's holdings in Mason and Kerr counties, Texas. About 1892, Light resigned and moved to Chickasha, Indian Territory, where he again began raising a few head of cattle. Thereafter, Light—who once had held full partnership in the largest of all the trailing operations—passed into oblivion.[37]

Charles Schreiner, on the other hand, weathered the financial storm. Although he did abandon the trailing industry in 1887, he continued to use company cattle brands, herds of livestock that he had acquired in the debt assumption, and the pastures he bought from Light. His overall investment in the cattle trade increased rather than decreased. In addition to his extensive mercantile operation, Schreiner soon came to control banks, became a pioneer in the field of mohair production, and eventually acquired some 600,000 acres of ranchland in the Texas Hill Country. By the time of his death, on February 9, 1927, Schreiner was one of the state's wealthiest citizens.[38]

But Charles Schreiner's success is a relatively well-known example of Gilded Age enterprise in Texas; less publicized, but just as dramatic, was the financial recovery of John T. Lytle. Although relieved of the trailing concern's considerable debt in 1887, Lytle continued for a time to experience reverses. Broken by the near-bankruptcy, Thomas McDaniel died that year, and Lytle, undoubtedly dejected, returned to his ranch near Castroville. He had lost his partner, relative, and friend when McDaniel died. Perhaps because of this, along with the failure of the transportation agency, Lytle decided to divest himself of much of the Lytle-McDaniel properties. In the fall of fateful 1887, he sold most of his personal holdings (estimated to have been almost 50,000 acres of land and several thousand head of livestock) for $400,000 to the American Cattle and Trust Company of Fort Worth and New York.[39]

Even though Lytle had been active during the period 1871 to 1887 in the Lytle, McDaniel, Schreiner, and Light Cattle Company, he had simultaneously made other significant investments in the cattle trade. In 1881, in partnership with A. Conkle of Kansas City, with whom his transportation agency occasionally associated in trailing contracts, as already described, Lytle had organized the original Rocking Chair Ranch in Wheeler and Collingsworth counties, Texas. In the fall of 1882, Lytle and Conkle sold this property—150,400 acres of land and 14,745 head of cattle—for $553,000 to what became the Rocking Chair Ranche Company, Ltd., of London. During the same period, apparently in partnership with McDaniel and a P. W. Thomson, Lytle had started the firm of J. T. Lytle and Company on a 41,462-acre tract of Maverick County, Texas, land where, according to Lytle's own estimates, the company grazed as many as 60,000 sheep each year. With McDaniel, Lytle acquired title to 17,500 acres of land in Medina County, Texas, and with McDaniel and Thomson, he bought another 13,188 acres in nearby Kinney County. At the same time, he originated the Seven D Ranch in Pecos County, Texas; probably because it contained the famed Comanche Springs, it was easily sold some time later to the England-based Western Union Beef Company. And in 1886, Lytle, George W. Saunders, Jesse Presnall, and William H. Jennings—all of whom were transportation agents—founded the Union Stock Yards Company in San Antonio. By 1887, Lytle had directed the investment of some $9,000,000 in the Texas cattle trade.[40]

Although he apparently sustained a severe financial loss in 1887 when Schreiner acquired total control of the trailing concern, Lytle did not diminish his activity in the cattle business. In spite of McDaniel's death and notwithstanding the sale of much of the Lytle-McDaniel holdings, Lytle continued for several years to operate the Lytle and McDaniel Cattle Company in Lytle, Texas. Also, he and Jesse Presnall, of the Union Stock Yards, bought and trailed an occasional herd to pastures in northern states and territories. Moreover, soon after selling the bulk of the Lytle-McDaniel properties to the American syndicate in 1887, Lytle invested in the company, was elected to its board of directors, and became general manager of its Texas holdings. Then, in 1889, he joined as a silent partner with Thomas Jefferson Moore, a Llano, Texas, cattleman–banker–erstwhile contractor, and with W. H. Jennings and J. R. Blocker, both of whom had recently dissolved their respective transportation agencies, to purchase a half-million-acre ranch (the Piedra Blanca) in Coahuila, Mexico. In 1891, Lytle retired temporarily to his Medina County Ranch. Then, ten years later, he was elected to the executive committee of the Texas Cattle Raisers Association (present Texas and Southwestern Cattle Raisers Association), three years later being named secretary and general manager, a position he held until his death on January 10, 1907.[41]

The Lytle, McDaniel, Schreiner, and Light Cattle Company, which Lytle organized, in the final analysis controlled no less than 15 percent of all the cattle trailed northward from Texas during the twenty-five years that followed the Civil War. Indeed, if ten years of that period in which the company did not even exist were also taken into account, the firm's real contribution to the movement of cattle would approach 30 percent. It was by far the largest and probably the most financially successful of all the businesses of its kind. If profit percentages experienced by other transportation agencies can be applied as well to this one concern, then its gross revenues easily surpassed a million dollars. Doubtless, the obvious success of the Lytle, McDaniel, Schreiner, and Light Cattle Company encouraged many other eager entrepreneurs to engage in the transportation phase of the range cattle industry.

Consummate Conservative Contractor: Eugene Bartlett Millett

3

SUCCESSFUL, enterprising businessmen—as a subspecies of humankind—are quick to seize opportunity, visionary in their perception of the future, unbridled optimists, and ever eager to pursue the elusive prospect of profit. Most of the cattle-trailing contractors exhibited these qualities, improvising and innovating with dash and finesse. Perhaps it was the novelty of their industry or the unconventional nature of their lives on a raw, untamed frontier that infected them with vigor. Whatever the source, it was an almost universal quality among transportation agents. A few, however, also displayed an inordinate degree of caution. For example, Eugene B. Millett, one of those Texans who pioneered contracting, was the epitome of conservative business practices. Resourceful and resilient, he was never impetuous; he profited substantially, nevertheless.

Eugene Bartlett Millett, the son of Samuel and Clementine (Bartlett) Millett, was born on April 25, 1838, in Washington County, the Republic of Texas. His father, following his graduation from Bowdoin College, had migrated from Maine to Mexican Texas and began teaching school in present Grimes County, then a part of Stephen F. Austin's colony. Shortly thereafter he met, courted, and in 1833 married Clementine Bartlett, the daughter of Jesse and Frances Bartlett, who also resided in the colony. When the smoldering federalist sentiment in Texas finally boiled, spilling over into bloodshed, Samuel Millett supported the Texans' secessionist cause. In 1835 he served with James Bowie, a man of questionable character who later gained immortality at the Alamo, in the so-called Grass Fight against the centralist Mexican army; and in 1836, Millett fought with General Sam Houston's victorious forces at the Battle of San Jacinto.[1]

Following the war, Samuel Millett returned to teaching, but in 1838 he petitioned the Republic of Texas for the first-class headright to which, as a resident of the country before March 4, 1836, he was entitled. The veteran was granted a league and a labor of land (4,605.5 acres) in present Harris County. He immediately moved his wife and two children to the property and began stock-raising and farming activities. Shortly thereafter, the erstwhile New England schoolmaster became a slave owner by purchasing a Negro woman to serve as nursemaid to the Milletts' children. But Millett apparently lacked sufficient business acumen to succeed, for by 1840 he had lost most of his land and had moved his family to Austin where he reentered the teaching profession. About 1848, the family for some unknown reason returned to what remained of its Harris County holdings, and Samuel reverted once again to stock farming. By then the Milletts had seven children, four boys and three girls, Eugene being the oldest.[2]

An incessant dreamer, Samuel Millett in 1849 was infected by gold fever. News of rich strikes in California sparked his interest. Then, when he received word that his brother Solomon in Maine had joined the gold rush, he determined to enlist in the frenetic movement west. Millett organized a party of like-minded wealth-seekers, paying most of the cost of outfitting the expedition from his own meager resources, and, to provide for his family in his absence, he leased a hotel in predominately German New Braunfels, Texas, for Clementine to run. The trek westward was arduous, supplies running low before the Texans had reached Death Valley and several of the men dying from the ordeal. Even though Millett reached the gold fields, his backbreaking labor panning for riches produced little more than subsistence. In 1851, defeated in his quest for wealth and lonely for his family, he sadly returned to Texas. Using his wife's modest profits from the hotel, Millett again moved his family in search of financial success —this time to Seguin, a small community sixty miles northeast of San Antonio. There he bought 160 acres of land and began farming. Samuel Millett, his adventurous spirit broken by repeated failure, thereafter remained at Seguin. Slowly over the years he

28

became more cautious and conservative, an attitude that eventually infected his oldest son.[3]

Young Eugene Millett was also incalculably influenced by his religious upbringing. His mother and his father both were devout Methodists at a time when frontier Methodism was synonymous with rural fundamentalism. They took their children to church each Sunday, read the Bible aloud in their home daily, and attended every revival and camp meeting within practical traveling distance. "Clementine, in particular, lived by a rigid code and tried to hold her children to a narrow path, forbidding them to play cards and dance. She tried to instill in their minds that cards, liquor, and dances were the Devil's instruments. She would destroy a deck of cards if she found one in the house."[4] A few youths, as they approach maturity, rebel from such rearing —as Eugene apparently did while still in his late teens; others absorb and reflect such a philosophy throughout the course of their lives. Some do both. Eugene Bartlett Millett, once he reached manhood, never gambled—either with cards or with his business.

In 1856, at the age of eighteen, Eugene Millett sought financial independence. As a youth he had worked after school on the family farm, earning a few dollars, and evidently had held some part-time jobs in neighboring Seguin. He saved his money to accumulate $350 worth of capital and was eager, as his father had once been, to make his fortune. Young Millett planned to travel to Mexico, buy horses there, and drive them back to Texas for resale. His father, by then openly pessimistic of such ventures, vehemently opposed the scheme. A heated argument accomplished nothing, save strain on family relations, and Eugene launched his enterprise without his father's blessings. Rebelliously eager to succeed, he rode to Nuevo León where he bought an unknown quantity of horses and, alone, drove them back across the border. In Texas he traded several of the ponies for a Negro slave. In an uncharacteristic moment of bravado, Millett told the slave that if he could sell him for $1,200, he would give the Negro $200, and the two, driving the remainder of the animals, set out for Seguin. While en route, Millett did sell the slave. When the black man balked at the prospect of leaving the youth for a new, unknown master—especially without the windfall he had been promised—the Texan gave him $25 and convinced the naïve Negro he had profited. Millett disposed of the balance of the horses soon thereafter, and, with a profit of about $1,500, returned to Mexico for more animals. He continued the business until 1860 when he took his accrued capital, bought a ranch near Seguin, and began breeding horses.[5]

When the Civil War began, Millett decided he could best serve the South by providing livestock for the war effort. While one of his younger brothers, Leonidas, readily volunteered for duty with an infantry company being recruited in Seguin and surrounding Guadalupe County, Eugene gathered horses for sale to the Confederate cavalry. In the fall of 1861 he delivered 1,500 mounts at Prairie Marmon, Louisiana. He was advised by military authorities there that the army also needed slaughter cattle. Upon his return to Texas, he bought several hundred Longhorns and before the end of the year drove them to Louisiana for sale. Millett apparently was in the process of collecting more animals in the spring of 1862 when news of Leonidas's death reached him. Perhaps it ʼwas some intense feeling of guilt associated with his brother marching off to war while he remained safely at home, profiting, or even some vague, romantic idea of revenge that propelled him into the conflict; whatever it was, it led him to recruit a company of cavalry from the Seguin region. Organized in April as Company B, Thirty-second Texas Cavalry (Wood's Regiment), with Millett as second lieutenant and executive officer, it patroled the coastline of Texas for the duration of the war, Millett eventually rising to the rank of captain and serving as the company commander.[6]

Paroled at San Antonio in August, 1865, Captain Millett returned to what remained of his Guadalupe County ranch. His father, who had remained there to supervise operations, had died in 1863, and the spread's livestock had irrecoverably scattered. By the spring of 1866, Millett had located and sold merely $850 worth of animals that bore his brand. About then he happened to meet Alexander Ewing of San Antonio who had formed a partnership with Colonel J. J. Myers of Lockhart, Texas, for the novel purpose of selling cattle to northern buyers operating in Missouri. Ewing and Myers had invested all their available capital in acquiring the herd and consequently had no funds remaining to finance the drive northward. Millett, apparently rejecting their offer of a full partnership in the speculative enter-

30

prise, agreed to underwrite the cost of the drive to Missouri and even to supervise its actual delivery. Ewing and Myers guaranteed to pay Millett an undisclosed fee for his service.[7]

Planning to dispose of the Ewing-Myers herd at Westport, Missouri, Millett departed the Myers ranch at Lockhart in March, just in time for the 500-head herd to encounter a rain-swollen Red River. Eventually, Millett and his employees combined their animals with those of other trail herds also thwarted by the swirling torrent and, by creating a near-stampede, drove the reluctant cattle across. Two and a half weeks later, Millett reached the southern boundary of Missouri only to clash with irate farmers, who feared their livestock would be infected by Texas fever, and a sheriff, armed with an 1861 Missouri statute that forbade the importation of "diseased livestock." As Millett could not prove conclusively that the herd under his supervision was fever-free, he was ordered to turn about. Seemingly stymied, the Texan retreated a few miles, turned eastward through northern Arkansas, and, once across the Mississippi River, proceeded northward to Cairo, Illinois, where most of the animals were sold—notwithstanding considerable concern even there over the health of the Longhorns. By the time Millett had marketed all the livestock and returned to Texas, it was late fall. He cleared $2,600 for half a year's work, but he was convinced that trailing was far too arduous, impractical, and dangerous to justify his continued role in it.[8]

The northern market, located as it was in a quarantined area, made trail drives a risky endeavor in which the cautious captain refused to engage. In 1867, while a few Texans drove approximately 35,000 cattle northward—for the most part disposing of their livestock in north-central Kansas at a new railhead-market, Abilene—Millett gathered a mixed herd of horses and mules, drove them eastward to Louisiana and Mississippi, and reportedly sold them for a "small profit." Upon his return to Texas, he learned of Abilene. Joseph G. McCoy, an Illinois cattle buyer, in 1866 had conceived the novel idea of a centralized livestock market in Kansas for the Southwestern range and ranch cattle industry—away from the settled areas where drovers invariably ran afoul of local quarantine laws. After considerable difficulty, McCoy convinced both the Kansas Pacific and the Hannibal and St. Joseph railroads to cooperate with the scheme. He then located stock pens at the village of Abilene where cattle trailed there could be shipped eastward over the Kansas Pacific to the Missouri River and, once transferred to the Hannibal tracks, on to Chicago packing houses. Texas newspapers carried glowing articles about the new market. Drovers who utilized McCoy's facilities in 1867 were generally pleased with the results and freely said so. Millett, encouraged by the reports, resolved to drive a herd to Abilene the following year.[9]

That winter, the Texas cattleman slowly and carefully began selecting a herd for northern delivery. He bought only the best animals available, those which could best withstand the drive and would bring premium prices at the Kansas railhead. By early spring he had collected between 500 and 950 head of cattle, and launched his drive, moving slowly lest the animals lose an inordinate amount of weight en route. The sixty-day-march—frequently negotiated in merely forty days by more flamboyant trail bosses—brought Millett to Abilene in late spring, well ahead of most of that year's drives. There, he checked into McCoy's Drovers' Cottage to await buyers. It was a short respite. The Abilene promoter himself bought 224 of the Longhorns for resale, and shortly thereafter, Millett sold the remainder of the herd, netting $3,500.[10]

Profitable trail drivers—unimpeded by irate farmers, quarantine measures, or difficult topography—appealed to Millett. Upon his return to Texas, he invited both his younger brothers, Hiram and Alonzo, to join him in an expanded enterprise. They readily accepted his offer of employment. That winter, the three solicited cattle for the trail, some of which apparently were purchased outright by the Milletts and some simply were contracted for northern delivery. All told, the Millett brothers drove two herds to market during the spring of 1869. Hiram and Alonzo took one 3,000-head herd to Abilene for sale.[11]

The captain took charge of the second bunch and—in what at first blush appears to have been a rare aberration of speculation—drove about 1,000 animals northwestward to Argenta, Nevada, for sale at premium prices to miners. Millett had learned of the abnormally high Nevada demand for slaughter cattle while in Abilene the year before. Convinced that his information was correct and that the venture was not a gamble, he quickly capitalized upon the opportunity, netting $6,000 on the drive and subsequent sale. After he disposed of the cattle, Millett entrained for a holiday in San Francisco. There he happened to meet Andrew Drumm and William K. Shaefer, erstwhile miners from Ohio who had turned to ranching. Millett's revelation of the profit potential in the cattle-trailing business led them to propose a merger. Shaefer suggested that the Ohioans provide Millett with $100,000 of working capital. With it, the captain could buy thousands of Texas Longhorns, hire hundreds of drovers, procure scores of wagons and tons of supplies, and drive a continuous stream of animals wherever a sale could be concluded satisfactorily. Profits would permit further expansion of the enterprise, and Drumm, Shaefer, and Millett eventually would come to control the cattle-trailing industry—making millions of dollars for themselves in the process. The circumspect Millett rejected the idea immediately. The magnitude of the risk was simply too great. Parting as friends, Drumm and Shaefer returned to their ranches and Millett to his own firm of manageable proportions.[12]

Following the pattern he established in 1869, Eugene Millett in 1870 drove two herds to market. The Millett brothers, proceeding in tandem up the Chisholm Trail, sold the first bunch of 1,200 head at Abilene. The other herd was bossed by Alonzo westward to Nevada and marketed there to miners. Net income for the year's efforts totaled $12,000.[13]

Millett's profits in 1870 were not unusual, for most drovers that year unloaded on a seller's market. As a result, other eager businessmen joined in the activity and drove cattle northward in 1871—until almost 600,000 head had been trailed to Kansas for sale. Vastly oversupplied, the market for stocker, feeder, and slaughter cattle plummeted precipitously. The Milletts likewise transported livestock to Kansas that year, stopping off at Newton on the Santa Fe Railroad, a point some sixty miles closer to Texas than Abilene. Finding the price for Longhorns far below the cost of raising and trailing them, Eugene Millett considered driving his animals on west to Nevada, as several other contractors were forced to do. Then he learned that J. W. L. Slavens and M. B. George, Kansas City commission merchants, needed slaughter cattle delivered to various Indian reservations. Leaving his brothers in charge of the livestock, Millett entrained for Kansas City, contacted the cattle buyers, and confirmed the rumor. Slavens and George offered the Texan a contract whereby, for $2.95 per hundredweight of delivered cattle, he would supply a half-dozen Indian reservations with slaughter animals. The price was excellent, but Millett was uncertain that he could handle the entire proposition. He countered by volunteering to sustain three of the reservations, one Santee and two Sioux, in the Dakotas. Slavens and George accepted the proposal, and the three men signed a contract.[14]

The Texan immediately telegraphed his brothers the news and advised them to make ready for the drive. By the time Millett reached Newton, the necessary hands and supplies had been procured, and the herd was ready for the trail. The animals were delivered as agreed, and the captain began inquiring of army officials the status of neighboring reservations. They informed him that the Cheyenne at Fort Sully and Sitting Bull's Sioux at Standing Rock Reservation together required more meat than did his present contract; moreover, it was evident that deliveries at two sites could be handled more efficiently than at three. Millett again returned to Kansas City and discussed the matter with Slavens and George. As it was very difficult then to guarantee sufficient slaughter animals for the reservations at a set price—cattlemen invariably selling their livestock at the railhead-markets for eastern consumption whenever the price rose above that which the government was willing to pay—both Slavens and George were eager to cancel their contract with the army and allow Millett to negotiate his own agreement. They even aided the Texan to secure a $25,000 line of credit at Kansas City's First National Bank.[15]

As Millett had secured an oral pact with the military in the Dakotas, he needed only the cattle. The enterprising business-man remembered an old friend, Major Seth Mabry of Austin. Mabry had returned to Texas after the Civil War and acquired a sprawling ranch in Kimble and Mason counties. By 1871, he marketed annually 5,000 head of cattle. Millett telegraphed the major, laying before him the news of his contract and proposing that Mabry join with him in the operation. By wire, Mabry eagerly agreed to the proposed partnership and added that inasmuch as he was leaving for Topeka on business anyway, Millett should join him there where they could work out the details; meanwhile, he (Mabry), who apparently because of depressed market prices had not attempted to sell any of his livestock that year, would immediately send several of his herds northward to

34

Newton for Millett to use in fulfillment of the contract. The cattle were received by Millett's employees who drove them on northward to the reservations. It was late winter before all the animals were delivered.[16]

Millett and Mabry continued their business relationship for several years, expanding the operation in 1872 by trailing herds to Idaho ranchers, where Texas Longhorns then sold for $40 each, and to Ellsworth, Kansas, on the Kansas Pacific Railroad, where 6,000 Millett-Mabry cattle that year brought a relatively high $3.75 per hundredweight—an increase of $2.00 over the previous year's disastrous prices. By then, the partners (which apparently did not include Eugene Millett's brothers) were buying range and ranch cattle in Texas to supplement the supply afforded by Mabry's ranch. The following year saw similar tactics, for the businessmen drove herds to the Cheyenne and Sioux reservations, to Idaho, to Ellsworth—wherever the partners were reasonably assured of a profitable sale. Their net revenues in 1873, a year which saw prices for range cattle steadily decline, exceeded $35,000.[17]

The partnership profited primarily because Millett, unlike Mabry, scrupulously avoided uncertain ventures. But Millett on occasion would take a calculated risk. Once, when he and Mabry bought a herd of cattle in Texas for northern delivery, he ordered his drovers onto the trail in such haste to capitalize upon current high prices that the trail boss, L. B. Anderson, left without a proper bill of sale. Millett told the company employee that he, Millett, would personally bring the document to him as soon as possible. When the herd reached Red River Station, the ford of the Red River on the Chisholm Trail, a Texas Live Stock Association inspector stationed there to check north-bound herds for stolen cattle challenged Anderson's legal authority to drive the animals and raced pell-mell to the nearest town for assistance. Anderson simply drove the livestock across the river into the Indian Territory, out of the grasp of Texas officials, and made camp. Millett soon arrived with the necessary affidavit, satisfied the angry inspector that Anderson did have ample authority over the herd, and told his trail boss to proceed to market. Millett's cattle could have been impounded and embroiled in lengthy litigation—thereby delaying the marketing of the animals—had Anderson not had the presence of mind to cross the border. But

Millett was confident his trail boss could handle any possible situation.[18]

Mabry, however, was far from cautious. During the winter of 1872–1873, while Millett supervised the final delivery of contract cattle to the reservations, Mabry returned to Texas to buy livestock. Meeting with Millett in Ellsworth the following spring, the major announced that he had purchased several thousand Longhorns for speculation on the northern market. Millett, momentarily taken aback by the disclosure, objected vigorously. It was one thing to contract for the delivery of the bony bovines and quite another to sell the low-grade animals profitably. Millett insisted that Mabry extricate the partnership from the agreement, whatever the cost. The major went to Wichita where he was able to sell the Millett-Mabry title to the animals, losing $3,000 in the process. Severe though the loss was, the businessmen unloaded at an opportune time. Throughout the summer of 1873, the market value of range cattle steadily declined, reflecting both the relative quality of Longhorns and the impending monetary crisis that hit the nation early in the fall. Before the end of the year, Texas trail cattle sold for as little as $1.10 per hundredweight, a decline of more than 50 percent over the previous year's averages. Millett's caution probably saved the firm from bankruptcy.[19]

Millett's mounting disaffection with Longhorn cattle was far from transitory. During the winter of 1873 he visited several Idaho ranchers to whom he previously had delivered stocker animals. From a number of them he acquired 1,600 hybrid cattle, meatier than the rangy Longhorn but just as durable on a long trail drive. In the spring, joined by his brothers and his drovers, he herded the animals southeastward, apparently to Ogallala, Nebraska, where they were shipped on to Chicago. Millett accompanied his livestock eastward and personally sold them at the Union Stock Yards, his margin of profit reportedly increasing measurably because of the quality of the cattle and the method of marketing them.[20]

Millett by then seriously considered retiring from the gruelling, unnerving business of contracting cattle for delivery. For a cautious, conservative individual such as he, the speculative nature of his profession was an unending source of vexation. And his health was not good; indeed, while returning from Chicago to

36

Kansas in 1874 for a meeting with his business associate, Millett was forced to detrain at Omaha and consult a physician about a nagging pulmonary disorder. Advised to rest, he checked into a hotel where he was approached by James Lowe, a Southwest Texas rancher he knew only by reputation. Whether Lowe purposely sought out Millett or merely happened to meet him in Nebraska is unknown; it is clear, however, that Lowe sincerely desired to liquidate his ranch holdings. For $240,000 he offered to sell Millett and Mabry 20,000 mixed, short-horned livestock that he had bred over the years, the contractors accepting delivery at Lowe's Texas ranch. In his eagerness to dispose of the cattle, Lowe even agreed to accept 16 percent of the purchase price as down payment, the balance due after Millett and Mabry had sold the animals. Millett, deciding to risk all in one final trail drive, wired Mabry in Austin the news of the Lowe purchase and instructed him to approach Austin, San Antonio, and Galveston banks for financial underwriting. Millett would do likewise in Omaha and Kansas City. Too, he would afterward entrain for Washington to seek an expanded government contract that would enable them to supply all the Dakota Sioux with livestock.[21]

Apparently without much difficulty, Millett and Mabry secured the contract, agreeing to deliver several thousand steers (at $20 a head) and cows (at $12) to the Indians in the Dakotas. By securing the contract, Millett had removed the venture from the realm of speculation. Similarly, they obtained an undetermined amount of financial backing from each of the banks they approached. During the remainder of the fall, Millett and Mabry contacted other Texas ranchers, buying marketable livestock at an average price of $10 per head. By the spring of 1875, all told they had 52,000 cattle ready for the trail. The partners employed R. G. Head—an experienced trail boss who had worked for J. J. Myers, J. F. Ellison, and J. O. Dewees—to serve as general manager of the drive. While Millett and Mabry journeyed northward to sell the remainder of the animals, Head supervised the movement of some seventeen herds of livestock along the Western Trail to Nebraska. There the partners diverted individual herds—to Ogallala stock pens on the Union Pacific Railroad, to ranchers in the Northwest, to the Indian reservations—wherever it was necessary to consummate a sale. For example, the Texans sold 7,000 head to John W. Iliff, a Denver rancher-banker, who

37

was interested in crossbreeding experiments. Another 26,000 head were marketed to J. W. and George Bosler of Carlisle, Pennsylvania, who in turn sold the animals to the government for various Indian reservations. The expenses for the huge drive were much higher than usual, for it cost an average of $4 per head to deliver all the cattle; even so, Millett and Mabry in August, 1875, divided net profits of $100,000. They also dissolved their partnership.[22]

Millett, weary and in poor health, apparently made his final decision to abandon the cattle-trailing industry in 1875, after he had departed Texas for the northern market and his herds were en route to Nebraska; otherwise, it would be impossible to explain his personal purchase of 3,000 head of mixed Millett-Mabry trail stock at Ogallala. Hiram Millett was instructed to drive them back southward and place them on 3,000 acres of land Eugene owned in Baylor and Knox counties, Texas, and which were surrounded by open-range land. Millett had had enough of contracting and was determined to ranch instead. He soon bought another 12,000 head of cows and calves and, the following year, purchased eighty-six Durham bulls with which to improve the bloodline of his livestock. In late 1876, Millett bought a second spread, this one in central Kansas, near Ellsworth, along the Smoky Hill River. There he raised cattle and began breeding trotting horses. In 1881, he sold the Texas operation to the Hashknife Ranch and used the proceeds from the sale to improve his Kansas ranch. Meanwhile, he drove an occasional herd of cattle westward to Dodge City and reportedly sold several thousand head of slaughter beeves to the government for Indian reservations.[23]

But Millett for several years refused to live on either of his ranches, leaving the Texas spread for Hiram to operate and the one in Kansas for Alonzo. Eugene, at the age of thirty-eight, had married in 1876 and, after a few months' residence in Austin, moved his bride to a Victorian mansion in Kansas City. While his brothers raised horses and cattle, he dabbled in Kansas City real estate, became a landlord, and, with an A. L. Mason, bought a stern-wheel steamer, the *Ann Cade*, which ferried freight and passengers along the Missouri River between Kansas City and St. Louis.[24]

Trouble soon beset him. His horse-breeding operation was

far from financially rewarding. It was the economic drag that forced him about 1885 to sell his Kansas City home and investments and move to Idavale, his Ellsworth ranch named in honor of his wife. Meanwhile, he had purchased two small ranches in Texas, which Hiram and Alonzo managed, and these spreads were beginning to lose money. Northern quarantines legislated in the middle 1880s, as previously mentioned, forced down the price of all Southwestern cattle—making it impossible for Millett to dispose of his Texas livestock profitably. To save his Texas holdings, he mortgaged the Idavale. Then in January, 1886, cattlemen throughout the plains states were caught totally unprepared by a severe blizzard which blew southward out of Canada. Literally hundreds of thousands of cattle were frozen to death in the icy storm. Millett lost fully three-fourths of his Kansas livestock, many of them expensive, registered Durhams. He nevertheless tenaciously clung to his holdings. He borrowed more money—mostly on his reputation as a successful cattleman —to salvage his ranches. Slowly he began to recover, restocking his ranges and paying off his considerable debt. Then, in the Panic of 1893, his creditors called in all his loans. Unable to pay, Millett lost all three ranches in foreclosure proceedings. From the forced auctions that followed, Millett realized only enough money with which to buy a small ranch near Pomona, Franklin County, Kansas. There he raised trotting and quarter horses. In 1906, at the age of sixty-eight, Millett decided once again to raise cattle seriously. He bought a marginal spread at Laguna, New Mexico, and, leaving his wife and daughter behind at Pomona, moved to it. Soon thereafter, his wife died. Poor health, bad weather, and no capital defeated him. About 1915, his daughter, by then married to an Ellsworth rancher, pleaded with him to unload his unprofitable business and join her in Kansas. He did. Then in the fall of 1916, while traveling by train to Los Angeles to visit his sister, Millett died. He was buried at Ellsworth.[25]

Eugene Bartlett Millett, one of the first Texans to engage in the transportation phase of the range cattle industry, was also one of the first to abandon it. The business rested firmly upon speculation—either on prevailing market prices or on a drover's ability to traverse immense distances at a minimal cost. Such uncertainties weighed heavily upon Millett, forcing him in 1875 to revert to ranching, a business he sincerely, albeit mistakenly, believed to be far more secure. All told, and according to available documentation, he and his associates—at first his brothers and joined later by Seth Mabry—drove to market some 120,000 head of livestock. During the decade in which Millett's firm operated, it apparently cleared more than a half-million dollars for its owners. Compared with some of the energetic enterprisers who drove cattle northward from Texas later in the cattle-trailing era, Millett and Mabry played minor roles in the movement and sale of range and ranch cattle. Nevertheless, their business, which operated only ten of the twenty-five years in which livestock were trailed to market, accounted for more than 3 per cent of all the traffic in cattle. And during its heyday, the Millett and Mabry Cattle Company served as the standard of excellence by which all other contracting concerns were judged.

The
Family Enterprises 4

SEVERAL RANGE CATTLE transportation agencies—even
more than the Lytle, McDaniel, Schreiner, and Light Company
and Eugene Millett's firm—reflected the tendency toward the
family controlled business unit. Three of these, the Coggins &
Parks Cattle Company, the Blocker Brothers and Jennings Cattle
Company, and the Pryor Brothers Cattle Company, were among
the more successful of the cattle-trailing operations that flour-
ished in Texas during the latter half of the nineteenth century.

Moses J. Coggin, the son of Levi and Frankie (Lambeth)
Coggin, was born on January 14, 1824, in North Carolina. Seven
years later, his younger brother and future business partner,
Samuel R., was born. The boys' father, a marginal tobacco farmer,
in 1836 moved his wife and nine children to Marshall County,
Mississippi, and began growing cotton. In 1854, Moses and
Samuel left the family farm and migrated westward to Bell
County, Texas, where they established a moderately successful
freighting enterprise. The following year the brothers purchased
a herd of cattle, which they placed on a nearby leased pasture.
Within two years, the Coggins had lost fully one-half of the ani-
mals—to disease, the weather, and thieves.[1]

Notwithstanding their initial failure in ranching, the Coggin
brothers in 1857 sold their freighting concern, gathered what livestock remained, and drove them westward to a Brown County,
Texas, ranch they had acquired—a location then on the very edge
of the frontier. The following year they invested the proceeds
from the sale of their Bell County property in 3,000 head of
Longhorns. In 1860, for some unknown reason, they shifted their
ranch westward into adjacent Coleman County. Although their
method of marketing cattle before the Civil War has not been
uncovered, they were reputed to have been "unusually succesful

cattlemen." When the Civil War erupted, they sold their ranch to a neighbor, and both brothers volunteered for duty with Confederate forces. Unfortunately, nothing of their service in the conflict is known.[2]

After the war, the Coggins returned to Texas. For two years their activities were lost to records; whatever they may have been, they yielded the brothers sufficient capital in 1868 to re-enter the cattle trade. They repurchased their old Coleman County ranch and began restocking their range, primarily with Longhorns. About the same time, a San Saba County cattleman, W. C. Parks, moved his ranching operation and 4,000-head herd northward into Coleman County. The three soon met. Parks suggested a partnership, which resulted in the creation of the Coggins & Parks Cattle Company; the firm would raise cattle and drive its own herds northward to market. By 1870, the businessmen also contracted for the delivery of their neighbors' livestock at the railhead-markets. Within another three years, the company had changed tactics and had begun to buy all the animals it trailed to market, thereby substantially enhancing the firm's profit potential. And, if a profit could be made conveniently, the concern was ready to forego the trouble of a trail drive and dispose of its animals locally, as it once did when it sold its entire 3,000-head herd at Coleman to rival cattle contractor John S. Kritzer of Taylor, Texas.[3]

But Coggins & Parks ultimately became an unorthodox cattle-trailing enterprise, for it eventually came to rely relatively little upon popular Kansas railhead-markets for the sale of its livestock. The company in the early 1870s operated three ranches —in Brown, Coleman, and Concho counties. At first these ranges served as staging points for trail drives northward to Kansas. But Coggins & Parks suffered tremendously from Indian raids, and, to recover financially, the company about 1874 was forced to alter its business methods. In 1871, the firm had about 25,000 cattle ready for the trail to Kansas, and, for some inexplicable reason, was later than usual in placing its herds on the trail. The delay proved costly. A band of Comanches one night in July swooped down on Coleman County, where the Coggins & Parks cattle were being readied for the northward march, stampeded the animals, and drove an estimated 7,000 of them westward toward the forbidding Staked Plains. The businessmen immediately appealed to the military at Fort Concho for aid, and a troop of cavalry was dispatched in hot pursuit of the raiders. When the troopers returned late in the month, they were empty-handed; the Indians had force-driven the herd to the plains, killing along the way hundreds of the animals that could not keep up the pace. The military, then stymied by the uncharted *Llano Estacado*, had given up the chase. Coggins & Parks estimated the loss at $175,000.[4]

The problem with Indians was far from over. After rounding up what remained of their trail cattle following the Indian attack, the businessmen drove to market that year less than 18,000 head of cattle—only to find prices for range cattle severely depressed. No doubt perplexed by their dual misfortune, the Texans decided to move their breeding livestock from Brown and Coleman counties westward to their pasture in Concho County where, they reasoned, they would receive better protection from the military at Fort Concho. The Comanches, however, were far from intimidated by the proximity of the army post and in December swept through the area with a ferocity that equaled their summer foray. Coggins & Parks this time lost almost 6,000 livestock. Broken by the Indian raids and by the soft market of 1871, the company sold its Concho County pasture and disposed of most of the remainder of its cattle, about 8,000 head.[5]

For the Coggins & Parks Cattle Company, the trail-driving industry had been a disastrous experience. The entrepreneurs, nevertheless, did not abandon the trade in cattle. Instead, they returned to their Brown County range and again began breeding livestock, selling their marketable animals each year to contractors who operated in the area. Then, about 1874, they began driving cattle once again, this time to New Mexico where newly established ranchers were then paying premium prices for stocker animals. The drives—which passed through the heart of Indian country—were inordinately dangerous, but they were also unusually profitable. No doubt the businessmen by then were fatalistic about Indian depredations; and even though the Goodnight-Loving route to New Mexico was by far the most hazardous of all the cattle trails, the entrepreneurs were willing to gamble in order to recover previous losses. Profits from their initial drive exceeded $25,000—small in comparison with their earlier efforts but nevertheless a new beginning. By 1876, the partners not only

43

were trailing several thousand cattle to New Mexico each season but buying herds there as well, driving these animals on north to Colorado for resale. On some occasions they even trailed a few of the New Mexico livestock back to Texas to augment their own growing herds. Then, in 1880, the Coggins & Parks Company sold all its livestock for $103,000 to the Matador Land and Cattle Company and dissolved the partnership.[6]

The capricious nature of the cattle-trailing industry, profitable though it could be, apparently led the Coggin brothers and W. C. Parks to realize that it was merely a matter of time before they would be forced to sustain another, crippling loss—if not to Indians, then in the market. The Matador Ranch's eagerness to buy stocker cattle afforded the partners the opportunity to abandon the business with a profit, and they readily capitalized upon the situation. Parks returned to San Saba County and with his share of the proceeds from the liquidation purchased a ranch. The Coggins in 1881 returned to Brown County and in Brownwood established Coggin Brothers and Company, a banking house. They later opened a mercantile store and a flour mill in the community. Too, the brothers for a few years remained moderately active in the cattle trade. In 1883 they formed a temporary alliance with George H. Adams of Brownwood and Frank Collinson, an erstwhile buffalo hunter, purchased a 3,000-head herd of cattle, and drove them to Colorado for sale. Although this apparently was the Coggin brothers' last effort in contracting, they continued their interest in ranching. With Henry Ford, a Brownwood businessman who was associated with the Coggins' bank, and Collinson, the Coggins in 1888 established the Three Diamond Ranch in Brewster County, Texas. The spread was relocated near Midland, Texas, about 1894 and sold a few years later. The Coggin brothers thereafter, until their deaths shortly after the turn of the century, occupied themselves with their Brown County businesses.[7]

Even more active than the Coggins and Parks in the transportation phase of the range cattle industry, and consequently even more successful, were John, William, Abner, and Jenks Blocker. John Rufus Blocker, the eldest son of Abner (Ab) Pickens and Cornelia (Murphy) Blocker, was born on December 19, 1851, near Edgefield, South Carolina. The following year, the family moved to Travis County, Texas, where three more sons

44

were born to the Blockers by 1856. All four youths were educated in Travis County public schools, and John attended Texas Military Academy briefly when it opened in 1870.[8]

In 1871, John and William B. (Bill) Blocker established a small ranch in sparsely populated Blanco County and stocked it with some five hundred head of cattle. Although the brothers probably did not begin trailing livestock northward until 1873, a contemporary, E. C. Abbott, later recalled that they might have driven some Longhorns to market the same year they began ranching. It is certain that in 1873 the Blocker brothers acquired 3,000 head of cattle—some their own livestock, some purchased from area ranchers, and some contracted for delivery—and set out for Kansas. By the time the herd reached the northern railhead-markets that fall, the Panic of 1873 had caused prices to decline severely. The brothers were forced to sell prime slaughter beeves for $13 a head—far less than what they had anticipated.[9] The cattlemen were not discouraged, however; John Blocker later recalled that he was determined to get his cattle "to where the demand existed."[10] For the next twenty years, few contractors were more successful.

The business became a true family enterprise. Twenty-year-old Ab, who had remained on the family farm to help his widowed mother, was most eager to join his older brothers. After a particularly backbreaking year of picking cotton, which sold for four cents per pound, he announced to his mother that he was through with farming. Apparently in all seriousness, he later recalled, "I got down on my knees and promised God Almighty that if I ever planted another cottonseed I would first boil it for three days so as to make sure it would never come up."[11] By the time Ab had reported for work on the Blanco County ranch, his brother Jenks likewise had joined the firm. Although Ab and Jenks never rose to the rank of partners in the operation, loyalty was a company (and family) trademark. Once when John and Bill rode out from Dodge City to inspect a herd of 2,500 cattle that Ab had trailed northward, Ab turned in his saddle and said, "Johnnie, if you and Bill had 10,000 like that in the Chupadero country, we'd be sitting purty, wouldn't we?"[12]

During the first few years, the Blocker brothers relied chiefly on contract delivery of livestock for their profits. They would contact northern stock raisers and cattle buyers and receive from them firm orders for a specific number of Texas livestock. It was a relatively simple matter, then, for the Blockers to approach Texas ranchers and secure from them ample cattle with which to fulfill their contracts. Although information is sketchy, it is apparent that even in the beginning the brothers were more interested in buying the livestock they drove than in the less profitable yet less risky business of serving as mere transportation agents.[13]

In 1874, the company streamlined its operation by hiring cattle buyers. Their first such scout, William Henry Jennings of San Antonio, proved to be a valuable addition to the firm. Jennings, the eldest son of Joseph Pulliam and Susan (Crunk) Jennings, was born on March 24, 1851, in Tippah County, Mississippi. The Jenningses moved to Guadalupe County, Texas, in 1858 where they acquired a small ranch. Following the Civil War, Joseph Jennings began trailing his marketable cattle northward for sale, and William accompanied his father as a drover. By 1871, twenty-year-old William was an experienced hand and that year trail-bossed his father's cattle to Wichita. Then, for the next three years, he served in a similar capacity for cattle-trailing contractors J. F. Ellison and J. O. Dewees. By the time Jennings joined the Blocker brothers in 1874, he was an expert cattleman.[14]

Jennings was well acquainted with the cattle trade and with the types of livestock needed for the trail. During the winter and early spring, he traveled from ranch to ranch, buying animals for the firm and gathering herds, which the Blocker brothers then drove to Kansas and elsewhere for sale. Jennings was so adept at his job that in 1880 he was taken into the business as a partner. F. M. Polk was hired in 1881 to assist Jennings; the newcomer was kept busy throughout the spring searching out beeves that the company could drive northward for delivery. After the cattle had been purchased or contracted, Polk then joined various of the Blocker Brothers and Jennings Company's herds and aided in the receiving of the animals, seldom more than three hundred from any one rancher.[15]

Too, expanded business called for more systematized methods of trailing operations. Unlike some transportation agencies, the Blocker Brothers (and later the Blocker Brothers and Jennings) Company could rely upon militantly loyal family members to oversee the actual, tedious task of driving livestock to Kansas markets and northern ranges. During the first several years, when the concern's operation totaled only a few herds each season, each of the brothers—John, William, Abner, and Jenks—undertook personally the responsibility of trail-bossing the Longhorn cattle. By 1881, however, with the company contracting and buying more animals than ever before, the partners were required either to oversee operations in Texas or to station themselves at the railhead-markets to negotiate final sales and deliveries—and not personally to boss the drives. One Blocker Brothers and Jennings employee recalled years later that in 1881 the combine had no less than ten and possibly as many as fifteen herds (perhaps 45,000 cattle) following the hoof-worn trail to market. Hence, it was physically impossible for the owners themselves to direct each individual drive. Usually, in these large undertakings, several herds would be readied for the mass march and trail bosses secured for each bunch. Jenks or Ab would be detailed to oversee the entire operation, which, on occasion, could consist of 25,000 animals in as many as seven to ten herds. Their task was not to boss but rather to see that no herd loitered or followed a grassless path.[16]

This technique could be inordinately demanding on the overseers. In 1885, Ab was directed to deliver 2,500 head of cows and heifers to the newly established ranch headquarters of the Capitol Freehold Land and Investment Company, which had acquired from the State of Texas some 3,050,000 acres of land for having constructed the capitol building in Austin.[17] Eager with youthful exuberance to be the first to deliver cattle to the new ranch, Blocker quickly gathered the livestock in Tom Green County and set out northwestward across dry, largely uncharted plains, and he beat by several days his closest rival, Joe Collins, who bossed a herd being delivered by cattleman George West. At Buffalo Springs, in Dallam County, the ranch foreman, B. H. (Barbeque) Campbell, received the cattle and, as was customary, requested the drovers' assistance in branding the animals. Campbell had been unable to devise a mark that thieves could not alter. "It's got to be run with a straight iron, and it's got to be one rustlers can't burn over," he confided to Blocker.[18] The trail boss, eager to return to the trail but delayed by the lack of a brand, pondered the problem for a moment and then, with the heel of his boot, scratched XIT in the dirt. It was settled, and Blocker's

47

crew began marking the cows with what was to become one of the best-known cattle brands in history.[19]

It was July, still early in the trail-driving season, when Blocker left Buffalo Springs. He and his drovers gathered the remuda and moved northward to Las Animas, Colorado, where the horses were sold, and then boarded the Santa Fe for Kansas. When Blocker detrained at Dodge City, a telegram awaited him. His brother, John, instructed him to buy a horse, ride south until he met several Blocker-Jennings herds en route to Kansas, and divert them to a Deer Creek, Colorado, rancher identified only as "Mr. Robinson." Ab caught the southbound stage to Camp Supply, Indian Territory, where he secured a horse. A short ride farther south brought him into contact with the first company drive. When the cattle were turned west through the present Oklahoma Panhandle, local squatter ranchers stopped them with barbed-wire fences. The Oklahomans claimed the animals carried Texas fever, and they adamantly refused to permit passage of any trail herd from South Texas for fear of losses to the disease among their own cattle. Ab quickly sent word to John, and both John and Bill Blocker, along with Texas cattleman George West, who also had livestock stalled at the edge of the Panhandle, soon came to investigate. John Blocker and George West, according to Ab, hurriedly rode back to Camp Supply and spent approximately $60 on telegrams to Washington to secure relief. Finally, the Department of the Interior, which exercised authority over the Indian Territory, advised the cattlemen to cut the wire and proceed. It also ordered the cavalry to stand by in case of trouble. Once the news was received, Ab took a hand ax and chopped down the single strand of barbed wire that blocked the path. "It was some sight," he later reminisced, "to look back as far as the eye could see, nothing but cattle, cowboys, and chuck w[a]gons all hustling to cross 'the strip' which belonged to no one but was claimed by so many."[20]

About a week later, Ab Blocker, accompanied by his brother Bill, arrived at Robinson's Deer Creek ranch with the consignment of livestock. Once the animals were counted and the purchaser satisfied as to quality and quantity, Bill departed for Denver, leaving Ab to attend to final delivery and branding. As the overseer's horse was jaded, he borrowed a fresh mount from the rancher. When the animal was gored to death by a steer,

Robinson and Blocker exchanged heated words. Finally, the cattle were delivered, and Ab Blocker hustled his men off Robinson's land. Outside the fence, he unsaddled, dropped his gun belt, and called his drovers together. He admonished them, "Now boys, I'm going to sleep, and the first d[amne]d man that wakes me, I'll kill him."[21] That season, Ab personally supervised the delivery of more than 25,000 head of livestock, and he was merely one of several overseers employed by the firm.[22]

Even though the Blocker Brothers and Jennings Cattle Company grew to become one of the largest of all the trailing concerns, it usually maintained an excellent rapport with its employees. The firm did demand a full day's work for a day's pay, but such was common throughout the cattle-trailing industry. John Blocker was widely known as a harsh taskmaster; yet his employees frequently joked about the stern side of his personality. One drover reminisced that when he worked for the company, he could always count on "two suppers ever night . . . one after dark and the second befo' sunup next mo'nin'."[23] Blocker's austere façade sometimes caused anxiety among his hands. G. M. Carson recalled an illustrative episode when he worked for the outfit during the spring of 1879:

> One day while engaged in branding, a four-year-old-cow refused to go into the chute, but made a run for Ab Blocker, who lost no time in climbing to the very top of the high fence. She then turned in my direction, and I downed her with a stone which I threw with all my might. I thought I had killed her, and I felt I would be given a hasty discharge. I looked around to see Johnnie Blocker standing near, and he said in a very pleasant way, "Don't throw rocks at the cattle, boys," and I knew right then that my job was still secure.[24]

Most of the employees realized that beneath his cold, callous exterior, Blocker was a warm, personable individual. The story repeated most often by his drovers to characterize the real Johnnie Blocker took place in 1875 or 1876. A Blanco County, Texas, widow with four children had gathered her marketable steers, some one hundred animals, and tried to sell them to the cattleman for whatever he believed was a fair price. Blocker candidly informed her that he did not have enough cash to buy them outright; he could pay her, however, when he returned from disposing of them in Kansas. She then offered the animals for a mere $10 per head—if he would but pay cash for the steers. Blocker rejected the potentially profitable deal and put the livestock into one of his herds, promising faithfully to bring back the money. That fall, the transportation agent returned and handed the woman $1,500 in gold coin. When she started to pay him the going rate for having driven them to market, he refused saying, "The boys did not know they were in the herd."[25] And Jenks and Ab, all the other men noticed, received little preferential treatment, just because they were his brothers. Ab once lamented that he got "d[amne]d tired" of the menial tasks to which he was assigned.[26]

If Blocker-Jennings employees could say any one thing about working for the firm, it was that seldom—if ever—were things merely routine, for the concern usually delivered many herds each year. Sometimes, as in 1876, cattle were driven no further than nearby Texas points, but not infrequently Blocker Brothers and Jennings Cattle Company deliveries were made as far north as Pine Bluff, Wyoming. Cattle were even sold to Texas operators, such as S. M. Swenson and Sons, for their Dakota pastures; some herds were trailed no further north than the Indian reservations in present Oklahoma. The range and scope of the organization's business activities even included the buying of trail herds that had been transported northward by rival concerns. When in the fall of 1879 this did occur—several thousand livestock being purchased at Dodge City from the Lytle, McDaniel, Schreiner, and Light Cattle Company—the animals quickly were resold for a substantial profit.[27]

Through the buying, selling, and transporting of Texas Longhorns, the Blockers' company handled a considerable proportion of the total number of livestock that were trailed northward during the latter half of the nineteenth century. At the very least, the concern handled 122,000 cattle between 1871 and 1893,[28] or about 3 percent of all the range and ranch cattle traffic. This figure appears, however, to be a gross underevaluation of the company's activities. Certain sources credit the Blocker Brothers and Jennings operation with more than 330,000 head of livestock driven northward during the period,[29] or about 7 percent of the total traffic. One authoritative and credible source states that Ab

50

Blocker himself supervised the delivery of no less than 250,000 cattle. It seems reasonable to conclude that his work represented a fraction, no more than one-half, of the Blocker-Jennings total, which—all told—accounted for perhaps 10 percent of the entire range and ranch cattle traffic.[30]

The Blocker operation grew and prospered, at least in part, because the company—and especially its co-founder, John R. Blocker—had an excellent reputation for honesty among the cattlemen it served. Once, when John Blocker's business ethics were attacked by a rival company, XIT ranch manager B. H. Campbell steadfastly defended the transportation agent. Campbell noted that the Capitol syndicate was most pleased with the way Blocker's company had fulfilled its contract with the ranch. In Campbell's opinion, "Mr. Blocker's character is untarnished."[31]

But like most of the trailing companies, the Blocker Brothers and Jennings Cattle Company's reputation alone could not enable it to survive the decade of the 1880s. Quarantines, more than anything else, destroyed the concern's reason for existence. Although the firm unflaggingly clung to trailing as the best method of cattle transportation, driving herds northward to the Dakotas as late as 1893, the operation after 1885 turned primarily to ranching, which became its economic mainstay. The partnership itself did not even survive until the turn of the century, for by 1900 John ranched alone near Eagle Pass, Texas. When he died on December 1, 1927, Ab managed his ranch. The old trail boss remained there until his death in 1943.[32]

There also were other family groups that capitalized on the transportation phase of the range cattle industry. As in the case of the Blocker Brothers and Jennings Cattle Company, whenever a family enterprise evolved, some diversification could be expected, and, inevitably, one member of the firm emerged as the driving force behind the company's success. In the case of Pryor Brothers Cattle Company, Isaac Thomas (Ike T.) Pryor was the guiding genius.

Ike T. Pryor, the son of David and Emma Almira (McKissack) Pryor, was born on July 22, 1852, at Tampa, Florida. His father died there three years later, and his mother moved her three sons, of which Ike was the youngest, to live with a sister in Alabama. Mrs. Pryor's death in 1857 led to the separation of her children, Ike, then age five, being sent to live with an uncle, Orville McKissack, in Spring Hill, Tennessee.[33]

Bitterly unhappy with the status of an orphan in his foster home, Pryor ran away in 1861, quickly attached himself as a newsboy to the Army of the Cumberland's Third Ohio Cavalry, and witnessed the battles at Chickamauga and Lookout Mountain. In 1863, an army surgeon, Dr. R. Wirth, concerned that the youth might be injured, sent Pryor to Ottawa, Ohio, where the doctor had lived before the war, but the boy soon resumed his Huckleberry Finn adventure by seeking out a married cousin, Mrs. John O. Ewing of Nashville, Tennessee, with whom he resided for the remainder of the conflict.[34]

In 1870, Ike's oldest brother, A. M. Pryor, who was moving to Texas, visited in Nashville. He painted a glowing picture of the opportunities in the Southwest and convinced his younger brothers, Ike and David, both of whom lived in Tennessee, to join him. The three separated upon their arrival at Galveston, and Ike soon was employed as a farm hand near Austin by Bill Cain at $15 per month. From where he labored, Pryor witnessed the seemingly endless parade of trail herds plodding northward to market. Perhaps it was the heat, or his low wages, or the supposed adventure the youth associated with men on horseback that encouraged him to abandon farming.[35] Whatever the precise reason, Ike T. Pryor "then and there formed a resolution to take to the trail the next year when my term of employment expired."[36] Thus began one of the most successful careers in the history of the cattle-trailing industry.

From sodbuster to cowboy was an easy transition for Pryor to make. In 1871 he apparently told his employer, "You can take your plow and go to hell,"[37] and set out to find work as a drover. Bill Arnold, a Llano County, Texas, rancher, soon hired him at fully twice what he had earned as a farm laborer. A subsequent cattle drive to Coffeyville, Kansas, proved to be a watershed in Pryor's life; during the six weeks it took to drive the 2,500-head herd to Kansas, he became convinced that he had found his life's work.[38] "I remember," he fondly reminisced years later, "how we used to point the tongue of the wagon in the direction of the North Star every night so we'd be sure of the direction in the morning."[39] He became totally and unashamedly enraptured with the life of a drover. The following year, apparently still working for Arnold, Pryor earned $75 a month trail-bossing herds to Abilene, Kansas, and Colorado.[40]

In 1873, Pryor was hired as a ranch hand on a Mason County ranch owned by Charles Lehmberg. Twenty-one-year-old Pryor so favorably impressed the stock raiser that by the end of the year the youth had been named foreman, earning a respectable $100 per month. The next year, probably because he was thoroughly experienced in such matters, Pryor trail-bossed Lehmberg's cattle northward for delivery to the government at Fort Sill. Toward the end of the fall, Lehmberg offered to sell his 77 Ranch and livestock—20,000 acres of land and 1,500 head of breeding stock —to Pryor, for the disastrous effects of the Panic of 1873 had broken the rancher's resolve to remain active in the cattle trade. Pryor leaped at the opportunity. Although he probably financed his initial business venture almost entirely with borrowed money, the extent of his indebtedness and the source of his backing have not been uncovered.[41]

Pryor soon was a most successful cattleman. Using his own marketable livestock, some 250 head, as the nucleus for a trail drive in 1876, he scouted neighboring ranches for additional cattle. Mason County rancher John W. Gamel accepted Pryor's offer to deliver for a set fee Gamel's 1,250 cattle on the northern market, and Pryor's career as a cattle-trailing contractor began. The drive terminated at Ogallala, Nebraska, and Pryor returned to Texas with sufficient profit to allow himself the luxury of a trip to the Centennial Exposition at Philadelphia.[42]

Upon his return to Texas that fall, Pryor saw the opportunity to capitalize upon local market conditions. Nearby Austin each autumn needed slaughter animals. He formed a partnership with Ship Martin, a Llano County cattleman, and on the first of each month, the two stockmen drove twenty head of beeves to Austin. As there was no stockyard, the livestock were delivered to a vacant lot just south of Colorado Street, where, in the open, butchers slaughtered the animals and dressed the carcasses. This commercial outlet for his steers soon enabled Pryor to accumulate the capital he needed to engage actively in the trail-contracting business.[43]

Pryor's prowess as a cattleman improved steadily over the next few years. Most of his attention during 1877 was focused on the Austin market; it was not until 1878 that he returned to the more lucrative business of contracting beeves for northern delivery. This time, gathering a herd of 3,000 head from his neighbors and from his own livestock, he set out for Kansas. The profits from that season reportedly were large and almost entirely financed his drives of 1879—some 6,000 animals. In 1880, Pryor ballooned into the status of a major transportation agent by directing the movement of no less than 12,000 head, or about one-third as many cattle as were being processed that year by the giant firm of Lytle, McDaniel, Schreiner, and Light.[44]

Beginning in 1881, Pryor supervised the delivery of as many as 40,000 animals each season. For those animals he purchased in Texas, drove to northern railhead-markets, and sold for himself, he realized a handsome $3 to $5 profit per head; and even for those that he merely transported for others, he cleared $1 to $2 per head. In 1881, Pryor formed a partnership with one of his brothers, A. M. Pryor, and hired his other brother, David, to manage his 77 Ranch.[45]

By 1884, Ike T. Pryor confidently believed that he could manage any number of livestock on the trail. He apparently spent the winter of 1883–1884 soliciting trail herds, because by early spring he had contracted to deliver, and purchased all told, 45,000 South Texas cattle. He moved them all in one monumental drive.[46]

The logistical problems of the drive were enormous. Pryor hired one hundred and sixty-five drovers, fifteen good cooks, and fifteen experienced, competent trail bosses. Six horses for every man (over 1,000 saddle ponies) were purchased; chuck and equipment wagons, one for each of fifteen herds, were secured and stocked with supplies. Thus—even before the cattle had been moved a single mile—Pryor had expended some $2,000.[47]

One of the fifteen 3,000-head herds was captained by Jeff Farr. Near Brady, Texas, an electrical storm stampeded the cattle, Farr's drive alone losing some five hundred head of beeves. The following morning, Pryor, riding in a "double buggy," reached Farr's campsite. Over a cup of coffee, the boss expressed pleasure in Farr's ability to retain control of the livestock, for, Pryor disclosed, most of the other fourteen herds had been lost altogether; it would take days to recover all the animals, Pryor correctly predicted.[48] Fortunately for the Texas cattleman, the rest of the drive was uneventful. Drover Jack Jones, who later reminisced

54

at length about the drive, recalled that the herds saw not "a living soul on that last 150 miles of the trip" to Dodge City. But, making an incredibly fine distinction, he acknowledged, "We saw plenty of Indians."[49]

All in all, Jones asserted in his own unabashed style, it was a pleasant passage:

> We had a nigger cook. All Ike's crews had nigger cooks. Why, no white man would have stooped so low as to cook [in] those days. Jeff said Ike fed better than any other trail man. I guess he did, [for] we had plenty of good grub. We had dried fruit, canned stuff and plenty of fresh meat. You know, it was the custom to pick up your eating meat. You couldn't eat trail stuff—would give you a fever. That's the honest truth. Jeff always rustled the eating meat. Wouldn't let no other man in our outfit do that job, either. Said it was his responsibility.[50]

Jones's explanation aside, it is doubtful that ranch cattle were rustled merely to provide fever-free meat for drovers; rather, it would appear that if indeed Farr did appropriate slaughter beeves along the way, he did so to reduce his shrinkage, thereby giving his employer more profit and, perhaps, himself a substantial bonus. Because of trail bosses such as Farr, Pryor's overall numerical losses in cattle that year were merely 3 percent, well within the range of acceptability insofar as profits were concerned.[51]

In Colorado, Pryor disposed of the first 4,000 steers to three Tennesseans identified only as the Baty brothers. It took five days for Pryor's men to brand the animals for the ranchers, but it was time well spent, for Pryor received some $62,000—$15.50 per head—for the stocker cattle. The remaining 41,000 animals were trailed on to Montana, Wyoming, and the Dakotas and were sold for similarly good prices. Of the $660,000 that the Pryor brothers received for the cattle, their gross profits were approximately $176,000. After all expenses were deducted—roughly $45,000—they netted a handsome $130,000.[52] Under ideal conditions, contracting was lucrative.

The Pryor brothers then invested their substantial profits in livestock, which they placed on leased pastures in southern Colorado. They fattened some 20,000 cattle annually, for three years, almost all of which were consigned to the St. Louis Canning Company. In spite of a severe winter in 1884–1885 and a general weakening of the cattle trade after 1884, the brothers averaged selling $65,000 worth of slaughter beeves each year. And this was supplemental to their cattle-trailing enterprise. But by 1886, the transportation phase of the range cattle industry, because of northern quarantines against Texas livestock, was suffering such a sharp decline that the Pryor brothers abandoned the business.[53]

Their problems had only begun. Perhaps foreseeing that the range cattle industry was about to undergo tumultuous change, the partners in 1886 seized the opportunity to dispose of their Colorado holdings to a Cleveland-based syndicate that was buying ranch property and breeding stock in the area. Once approached by the Ohioans, Ike Pryor entrained for Cleveland, arriving there in the fall. After several days of negotiating, he sold the Pryor brothers' operation for a figure somewhere between $500,000 and $600,000—the exact amount depending upon the precise calf-count the following spring. Pryor received $100,000 cash down payment and, no doubt pleased with his own business acumen, began his return journey to Colorado. He had reached Chicago when, on the morning of November 17, news reached him that a bitter blizzard had dumped eighteen inches of snow on his Colorado pastures. As far south as central Texas, sub-freezing weather caught cattlemen totally unprepared. In January, yet another storm hit. When the Pryor brothers in the spring proceeded to round up their cattle, only some $65,000-worth of pitifully poor livestock remained. They were thus unable even to meet the cash advance they had received. The storms cost them more than $500,000 in actual sales and left them $35,000 in debt. They liquidated their assets and ended their partnership.[54]

Ike Pryor was fortunate. He was eventually able to recover most of his losses. At the time of his near-bankruptcy, he also owed a St. Louis commission company some $30,000, which, after the winter of 1885–1887, he was unable to pay. A quick trip to St. Louis got him not only a desperately needed extension on the note, but as well an additional $70,000 loan, largely on his name and reputation as a cattleman. Pryor then invested in and was named president of the Texas and Colorado Land and Cattle Company, a concern that, ironically, operated exclusively on leased lands in the Indian Territory. By 1898, he had once again acquired a large herd of his own, and, immediately after the shooting had ended in the Spanish-American War, shrewdly shipped 8,000 cattle to strife-torn Cuba, where animals which brought $15 in the United States quickly were sold for $85. He climaxed his career by acquiring 100,000 acres of ranchland in Zavala County, Texas. By the time of his death, on September 24, 1937, Pryor was a millionaire and had served as president of the Texas Livestock Association (and later its successor, the Texas and Southwestern Cattle Raisers Association), the National Live Stock Shippers' Protective League, and the American National Live Stock Association.[55]

Cattlemen such as Ike Pryor, John and William Blocker, and Moses and Samuel Coggin were relatively common to Texas during the later half of the nineteenth century; their success stories are not very unusual. The activities of other family units that profited from the transportation phase of the range cattle industry could easily be added to this list. These businessmen were—first and foremost—cattle-trailing contractors who made money simply because Texas livestock needed to be driven northward. The contractors' precise business activity was probably as much fortuitous circumstance as anything else, for most of the men were opportunistic entrepreneurs, in the best tradition of the Gilded Age, who saw a need for a particular service, seized the opportunity, and profited substantially thereby.

Horizontal, Vertical, or Conglomerate 5

THERE WAS NO patent-medicine prescription for success—or for failure—in the cattle-trailing industry. Each businessman, association, and company operated solely to make a profit. However that end might be achieved (usually along ethical lines), it was a legitimate avenue of activity for the transportation agent. By definition, he was a middleman whose earnings came from performing a service, or from speculating on future prices by buying the cattle that he drove to market. Whichever method best suited him (or a combination of the two), he was frequently more businessman than cattleman (and more often speculator than manager), for his other, simultaneous investments frequently ranged the full breadth and scope of business consolidation—horizontal, vertical, and conglomerate.

Horizontal combinations, from the viewpoint of the cattle-trailing contractor, were the most logical. For example, the expansion of a concern could enlarge its capital reserve, thereby making it more active in its field and, consequently, more profitable. Considerations of this nature encouraged John Lytle and Thomas McDaniel to invite Charles Schreiner and John Light to invest in their operation. Transportation agencies seldom were single-owner businesses, for the very character of the activity—cattle strung out all the way from Texas as far north as Canada—was too demanding for one man to oversee efficiently or effectively. Colonel James F. Ellison, for example, found that within two years of his initial trail drive he was unable to continue in the trade without taking on an associate, his expansion being both horizontal and vertical.[1]

James F. Ellison was born in Winston County, Mississippi, on November 6, 1828, and moved to Prairie Lea, Texas, in 1850, where he became a farmer. During the Civil War he reportedly served with the Confederate Army, returning home in 1865 to a weed-covered farm that offered little financial future. In 1868, Ellison decided to brave the risks of a trail drive, for the profits at the end of the trail were lucrative. In this one drive Ellison was quickly metamorphosed from farmer to cattleman. He gathered 750 head of mixed cattle, largely on credit, and accompanied by his son and namesake and a few drovers whom he had hired with a mere promise of wages, set out on the Chisholm Trail for Abilene. Aside from a few minor problems with Indians in the Territory, who demanded beeves in payment for transit through their range, the Ellison venture experienced little difficulty. The herd was sold to a representative of a Chicago slaughterhouse, and the entire crew returned to Texas by way of the Mississippi River, New Orleans, and Galveston. "This trip proved to be a profitable one," Ellison's son later recalled. "After paying for the cattle as soon as he returned home, father had $9,000 cash, which was a lot of money in those days."[2]

Not surprisingly, Ellison continued in the trailing business. In 1870, he put an undetermined number of Texas Longhorns on the trail; the results doubtless brought profit, because the following year he began to expand this operation. That year Ellison was contacted by an old friend and comrade-in-arms, John O. Dewees, and offered what ultimately was a lucrative proposition.[3]

John O. Dewees, born on December 30, 1828, in Putnam County, Indiana, moved to Bastrop, Texas, in 1848, and engaged in farming and stock raising with his father. During the Civil War he served with Company B, Thirty-second Texas Cavalry (Wood's Regiment), but little of substance is known about his military activities. Following the end of the war, Dewees returned to agrarian pursuits, establishing a ranch in Wilson County, Texas, which he stocked with maverick cattle then readily available to anyone willing to gather them. By 1871 he had sufficient livestock on hand to offer them to transportation agent Ellison at a "reasonable" price. Two thousand Dewees cattle thus were contracted by Ellison who located a buyer for them near Ellsworth, Kansas. The animals marketed at two and one-half cents per pound, or some $50,000 all told. Both Ellison and Dewees profited handsomely and decided, therefore, to cement the relationship by forming a partnership, Dewees supervising the procurement of the livestock and Ellison overseeing the actual

60

transportation and sale of the animals.[4] In a very real sense, the new association amounted to a vertical combination—where the company controlled the operation from the raising of cattle to the ultimate disposal of them at the end of the trail.

The firm's horizontal tendencies—merger with other trailing concerns—were not dormant, however, during the next several years, for Ellison and Dewees[5] expanded their operation significantly. The company, between 1871 and 1882,[6] drove no fewer than 400,000 head of livestock to northern railheads and ranges.[7] At the very least, the outfit immediately after its creation began trailing an average of 20,000 to 40,000 Longhorns annually. In 1874, the company entered into a short-lived horizontal merger with the firm of Millett and Mabry. The combine that year processed no less than 100,000 head of cattle.[8]

Between then and 1882, when Ellison reportedly went bankrupt, the firm of Ellison and Dewees formed several other temporary alliances with various contractors and transportation agencies. The details of these arrangements, however, for the most part have not been unearthed. In 1875, for an example, the company of Ellison, Dewees, and Bishop operated out of San Antonio; three seasons later, the partnership—at least insofar as the last-named associate was concerned—no longer existed. A Dewees, Ervin, and Ellison Company also operated briefly during the same period, and James Ellison in 1878 joined with a James A. Sherill for the expressed purpose of delivering one herd to the northern market.[9]

The quest for profits led to many such horizontal and vertical combinations, some temporary and some permanent. The career of Karnes County, Texas, cattleman J. Monroe Choate is another excellent example. Born in Tennessee on April 28, 1822, Choate migrated to Leon County, Texas, about 1854. Two years later he moved his family of ten children to a farm along Hondo Creek in Karnes County. During the Civil War, Choate saw and seized the opportunity to enter the cattle trade. In 1862, he formed a partnership with a James Borroum and drove a herd of Longhorns to Mississippi where it was sold to the Confederacy. Although it appears likely that Choate and Borroum joined with each other in additional drives and sales during the war, evidence of this has not been found. In 1866, the two businessmen drove a herd to Iowa to locate a market; the size of the herd and the extent of their profits, if any, are not known.[10]

About 1870, Choate began associating with John (Pink) Bennett, a transportation agent from South Texas. Apparently the Bennett-Choate arrangement was a very loose relationship, like some of those entered into by James Ellison, whereby Bennett and Choate combined to transport livestock whenever the opportunity presented itself. Such business associations did not preclude one of the partners joining in a separate, albeit simultaneous, agreement with yet another contractor, as Choate occasionally did. Consolidations of this type by transportation agents were common.[11] Apparently, structural lines for these companies were very fluid; even members of the Lytle, McDaniel, Schreiner, and Light Company (collectively and separately), as it has been shown, occasionally joined in temporary mergers.

Such arrangements obviously were concocted if and when profits realistically might be expected to result therefrom; vertical combinations (and growth) by transportation agencies were common because they were considered potentially profitable by the participants. Colonel John J. Myers of Lockhart, Texas, whom Joseph G. McCoy credits with being the person who convinced him to establish his stockyards at Abilene, and a rancher who became a contractor, exemplifies this vertical pattern of business integration. From Myers's ranch, located eight miles north of Lockhart in Caldwell County, he organized drives using his own cattle and those he purchased from area ranchers. Beginning his trailing activities as early as 1866, Myers had so expanded his operation by 1869 that he was unable to supervise it all personally. That year he employed Richard G. Head, who later became general manager of the huge Prairie Cattle Company, to oversee the Myers trailing operation.[12]

Thereafter, for the most part, Myers ran his business from his Caldwell County ranch, sending out herds from his Lockhart headquarters. Unlike many operators during the period, Myers did not rely solely—or even primarily—upon the cattle markets at the northern railheads or upon the secondary demand for Texas cattle among northern stockmen. Instead, he frequently dispatched his herds across the Rocky Mountains for sale at Salt Lake City. He simply transported the livestock he raised and purchased to any point, observed Joseph G. McCoy, where a profit could be made. Had Myers not died in 1874, it is reasonable to assume he would have become one of the largest and most successful of all the transportation agents.[13]

Similarly, Abel Head (Shanghai) Pierce, who had ranched in Texas since before the Civil War, expanded his activities through buying South Texas cattle, which he in turn trailed northward for sale. The trailing era produced no more colorful character than Shanghai Pierce.[14] A large, portly man who rode a fine white horse, he apparently enjoyed living up to his colorful image and went out of his way to augment the folklore attached to his name. Whenever Pierce would ride into a cow camp to purchase animals for a northern drive, he invariably was accompanied by a Negro batman who led a packhorse laden with specie with which to buy the cattle. The show that Pierce staged for the benefit of wide-eyed, youthful cowboys left an indelible impression. George W. Saunders, who later achieved considerable prominence in his own right as a transportation agent, recalled his own awe at seeing Pierce "empty the money on a blanket in camp and pay it out to the different stockmen from whom he had purchased cattle."[15] Pierce, although moderately successful as a rancher-contractor, was merely a minor figure within the scope of the cattle-trailing industry; compared with numerous others, Pierce was only a small businessman who occasionally exploited the profits that trailing offered.

Among those others was Dillard Rucker Fant, the son of W. N. and Mary (Burriss) Fant, who was born on July 27, 1841, at Anderson, South Carolina. At the age of eleven, along with his six brothers and sisters, he moved with his parents to Goliad, Texas, where his father opened a mercantile store. Three years later, young Fant secured a job as a teamster, driving freight wagons between San Antonio and Goliad. During the Civil War, he served with the Twenty-first Texas Cavalry. Following his parole in August, 1865, he returned to Goliad and immediately engaged in stock raising. The size of his ranch and the extent of his operation are not known; it is known, however, that in 1869 he drove a herd of cattle northward for sale. Thereafter, his combined business activity—ranching and trailing—grew markedly.[16]

In 1866 Fant had begun limited operations in stock breeding and even sheep raising. His scope had so expanded by 1869 that he had sufficient marketable cattle (650 head) to justify a northern drive. The animals were marched to Omaha where they reportedly brought Fant a substantial profit. Thereafter, for the next several years, the Texan drove numerous herds of cattle northward for sale. Using his ranch in Goliad County as a base for his overall operation, he bred livestock, bought cattle from neighboring stockmen, and contracted animals for northern delivery. By 1872, Fant further expanded the scope of his business. That year he purchased some 1,200 horses, which he drove to Kansas for resale, disposing of them at a reportedly "good figure." Also in 1872, the entrepreneur trailed at least 2,000 steers to Wichita where they were sold. Within another three years, Fant was buying prepared herds from rival contractors, such as George W. Saunders, and driving them northward.[17]

In the decade that followed, Fant's road brands—the F and the ID—became fixtures on the cattle trails. In 1876, he sent at least twice as many cattle northward as he had the previous year. Then in 1877, for some inexplicable reason, he sold all of his trail cattle to contractor-rancher George West. And if he drove any animals northward in 1878, evidence of such activity has not been uncovered. But in 1879, Fant returned to the trail. He sent several herds to Dodge City and Ogallala; moreover, he furnished 4,000 steers to the Red Cloud Sioux Agency in the Dakotas. By 1881, Fant again was driving horses to Kansas for sale, and he continued his regular cattle-trailing activities. Indeed, in the 1880s, Fant expanded to the status of a major transportation agent, for his company averaged handling 40,000 animals a year between 1881 and 1885. In 1884, he controlled a drive of 42,000 head of Longhorns—22,000 of which were delivered to one cattleman, A. H. Swan of Wyoming.[18] And if Fant's margin of profit were similar to that of Ike Pryor and many of the other contractors, then his net earnings from that one year's drive easily exceeded $60,000.

All told, Dillard Fant transported and sold between 150,000 and 200,000 cattle, or 4 to 5 percent of all the trail traffic. Like most of the contractors who diversified their business, Fant did not rely solely upon the market demand at the Kansas railheads for his sales. In addition to driving cattle to Wyoming, as in 1884, the South Texan regularly delivered slaughter beeves to Indian reservations. By 1884, Fant was thus selling as many as 7,000 cattle each year.[19]

While Fant's trailing business expanded markedly each year after 1869, so too did his ranching operations. In 1874, he had begun selective cattle breeding, using both Hereford and Durham strains to improve the quality of the Longhorn livestock he offered for sale. During the 1870s and early 1880s, he also purchased additional grazing lands. He acquired almost a quarter of a million acres in Hidalgo County, Texas, at a site he styled the Santa Rosa Ranch. Soon thereafter, Fant bought 8,200 acres near Fort Worth in Tarrant County, 60,000 acres in Live Oak County, and 60,000 acres in Frio County. He also leased an additional tract of land in present Oklahoma. By the time of his death, on January 15, 1908, he was one of the largest ranchers in the Southwest.[20] For Dillard Fant it was logical to acquire large pastures on which cattle for the northern market might be raised. His vertical expansion, thus, allowed him greater profits, as evidenced by the overall growth of his business operations.

Vertical business structures were by far the most common manifestation of economic integration employed by transportation agents. Such was the method employed by cattleman George W. West. Born in Tennessee in the 1840s, West accompanied his parents to Texas sometime during the 1850s and settled in Lavaca County. About the time of the Civil War, young West acquired a small ranch in the western half of the county, near Sweet Home, and began raising cattle. Unfortunately, nothing of substance concerning his business activities is known until after the war. In 1866, West began gathering his own livestock and contracting cattle among his neighbors to be driven northward for sale. How many head he collected or how successful he was in this activity before 1871 is open to conjecture. But during the decade of the 1870s, West established himself as a substantial cattleman by operating his ranch in Lavaca County and by acquiring another 60,000 acres of ranchland in Live Oak County. Too, he continued driving cattle—some raised by him, some purchased, and some contracted for delivery—to Kansas. By 1874, when he merged his business with that of Willis McCutcheon, a South Texas transportation agent, West had trailed and traded an estimated 75,000 head of cattle to Kansas railhead-markets.[21]

If West was successful as a cattleman, it was because he was a careful businessman. His brother, Sol West, recalled his own experience in 1874 when he returned from trail-bossing a company herd to Kansas:

> Myself and the men got back to Lavaca County about December 1. My brother, George, was [also] the bookkeeper for the firm of McCutcheon & West, and when I turned over to him the list of my receipts and expenditures, and what cash I had brought back with me, he proceeded to figure up results. I had to check it very carefully to be sure he made no mistake. We had agreed on a price for the cattle when I started with them, and I was to have one-half of all they brought over that price, after deducting the expenses incident to the trip. The net profit on the year's work [on the drive and sale] was $1.50, and when my brother handed me the 75c he made some jocular inquiry as to whether I expected to buy a herd of my own, or start a bank with it.[22]

McCutcheon and West, however, profited from the sale of the cattle on the northern market. The drive itself was a disaster only because Sol West lost sixty-five horses from the remuda, thereby making the trip unusually expensive.[23]

By 1883, George West had dissolved his partnership with McCutcheon and associated himself with John Bennett, previously a partner of Monroe Choate. Together they purchased a ranch in Jackson County to supplement the supply of marketable animals produced on West's two other spreads. They also continued the time-honored practice of buying trail cattle from area ranchers. By 1885, the businessmen were driving northward as many as 75,000 head of cattle each season. Although the majority of their herds were transported to Dodge City, they also supplied other ranches, such as the XIT, with stocker cattle, and various Indian reservations with slaughter beeves. But in 1885, West abandoned the contracting business entirely, for quarantines effectively blocked the trails northward and ruined the transportation agent's operation. Thereafter, West reverted almost entirely to raising cattle on his several Texas ranches.[24]

Another example of the tendency toward vertical business expansion is the case of George W. Saunders, the son of Thomas and Elizabeth (Harper) Saunders. He was born on February 4, 1854, at Ranch, a small, unincorporated settlement on Lost Creek in Gonzales County, Texas. During the Civil War, while his father and two older brothers served in the Confederate Army, George, along with his younger brother, Jack, supervised the family ranch. George Saunders's first experience with trailing livestock came in 1864 when he agreed to allow a neighbor, George Bell, to drive twenty head of Saunders cattle to Mexico to exchange them for desperately needed supplies. When Bell returned, Saunders recalled, "he brought us one sack of coffee, two sets of knives and forks, two pairs of spurs, two bridle bits, and two fancy 'hackamores,' or bridle headstalls, for which he traded our twenty beeves, and we were well pleased with our deal."[25]

Following the Civil War, the Saunders family's cattle-trailing activities began in earnest. In 1867, the patriarch, Thomas Saunders, gathered a herd (size and origin unknown) and drove it from Goliad to New Orleans. Aside from the fact that the elder Saunders allegedly contracted rheumatism as a result of exposure on the journey, the family apparently gained little from the effort. Whatever the profits, George Saunders later reminisced, two of his brothers, Mat and Jack Saunders, had "caught the trail fever" and in 1870 drove a herd of Saunders animals northward for sale at Baxter Springs, Kansas. When they returned, their tales of adventure on the trip, George Saunders insisted, "filled me with a wild desire to go on the trail too."[26]

Saunders, then sixteen years of age, convinced his reluctant parents to allow him to hire out as a drover, and he talked contractor Monroe Choate into giving him a job. The tenderfoot was apprenticed to trail boss James Byler, who immediately cautioned the teenager against sleeping while on duty. The journey pulsated with excitement—stampedes that enlivened the march, Indians that threatened the herd, buffaloes that blocked the trail, and swollen streams that had to be crossed. Saunders, who was at an impressionable age, never fully recovered from his enchantment with what he believed was the romantic life of the drover. Even the return to Texas, he remembered many years later, was a thrilling experience. The remuda of some 150 horses were driven back southward by fifty drovers accompanied by five chuck wagons and five cooks. At the Washita River, the Texans encountered a flooded stream and were forced to construct a raft with which to ferry the horses and wagons across. Some of the

67

more daring drovers elected to swim the three-hundred-yard-wide torrent in order to take a safety rope across for the raft. One by one they failed and returned, Saunders reminisced, and finally his turn came. In true Horatio Alger fashion, Saunders swam it: "The boys realized I had succeeded in accomplishing a dangerous feat. I felt very proud of myself, and think I added several inches to my stature right there, for I was only seventeen years old, and had succeeded in an undertaking in which four stalwart men had failed, but I am willing to confess I could not have gone ten feet further in my exhausted condition."[27] If there had ever been any doubt before as to Saunders's future occupation, apparently none remained, for thereafter his life revolved almost entirely about the driving of livestock to market.[28]

Shortly after his return from Kansas, Saunders was employed to drive cattle to a meat-packing house at Rockport, Texas. Later, he worked for his father, selling the family's cattle to contractors such as J. D. Reed and Dillard Fant. During this period, he served in the state's militia as a member of the Minute Company of Refugio and even as deputy sheriff at Goliad for a brief period of time.[29]

By 1872, the youthful Saunders had begun contracting an occasional herd to northern markets. He was characterized by his employees then as being "a good boss and a hard worker."[30] The drovers further noted that the Texan was flamboyant. Saunders loved fine clothing and beautiful women; he once halted a trail herd long enough to make a social call on a girl friend who lived nearby. However successful his romantic activities, his business did not suffer from his divided interests. By 1874, he had purchased a ranch near Goliad on which he raised and fattened many of the livestock that he later sold on the northern market. In 1874, Saunders married Rachel Reeves of Refugio County and, six years later, when his wife's health began to fail, moved to San Antonio where she could receive better medical care. Unable to resume his mobile life as a rancher-contractor because of his wife's condition, he virtually abandoned the cattle trade for a brief period, buying several hacks and teams and operating a taxi service in the city. In 1883, Saunders's wife died and, accompanied by two small daughters, he returned to the Coastal Plains of Texas and to the trailing business. He bought horses and cattle—

whatever he believed would sell on the northern market—and drove them to Kansas.[31]

Once, to dispose of three hundred Spanish mares, which he had bought in San Antonio and trailed to Hannibal, Missouri, he literally staged a wild west show. Saunders advertised, "Wild Texas Ponies for sale at William L. Fry's Stables, with an Exhibition of Roping and Riding Wild Horses."[32] When the crowd began to assemble, Saunders announced to prospective purchasers that they might select the animals they wished; to hold their attention, he later admitted, "I told them the bronc riding would be the last act of the show but that they would not be disappointed."[33] Several head were bought at the outset, buyers choosing the animals they desired and Saunders sending his hands into the corral to rope the horses. When sales began to lag and potential customers began to leave, the Texan had an "outlaw horse" roped, saddled, and mounted by Anderson Moreland, one of Saunders's best riders and most experienced hands. Crowd enthusiasm immediately increased, and sales rose. Saunders disposed of fifty head at Hannibal. Leaving there, the Texan repeated the rodeo-sale at Pittsfield, Illinois, and at St. Louis.[34]

Thereafter, Saunders's career testifies to the fact that the entrepreneurial genius he demonstrated at Hannibal was no mere fluke. In the true image of the Texas wheeler-dealer, he bought horses and cattle, trailed them wherever was necessary to consummate a sale, and continued to make money. In 1883, he associated with Harry Fawcett, an Englishman, in the purchase of the Narcisso Leal Commission Company in San Antonio. In addition to buying horses and selling them to drovers who needed remuda stock, the partners apparently developed a thriving cattle-trailing business of their own. In 1884, being unable to dispose of a large string of horses to trailing companies, Saunders and Fawcett sold the commission company back to its original owners and, with their herd of unmarked Spanish ponies, began a horse-drive over the Western Cattle Trail to Dodge City. In all, some 15,000 horses were marketed at an average profit of $15 to $20 per head. With a total profit of almost a quarter million dollars, little wonder the partners for the next several years preferred horses to cattle.[35]

Thereafter, Saunders's horizontal growth accelerated considerably. In the summer of 1884, he bought two carloads of saddle

69

horses, delivered them to a buyer on the Pecos River in New Mexico, and returned to Texas with enough profit to finance a buoyantly optimistic foray into the rugged Guadalupe and Delaware mountains of far West Texas in search of a lost, hardrock gold mine. He abandoned prospecting in October and negotiated a contract with H. H. Hall, a Toyah, Texas, rancher, whereby Saunders would drive Hall's quarantine-blocked cattle, some 2,000 heifers, to Luna Valley, Arizona, for a substantial fee.[36] Saunders later recalled that "the weather was getting cold, and the route was through old Geronimo's band of [Mescalero] Apaches, and I knew I would have a hard trip."[37] "Remarkable as it may seem," he asserted, "I lost only five head of those cattle on the entire trip, which were bogged in a marsh at La Luz."[38] That being the third herd Saunders personally had delivered that season, he decided not to assume any additional contracts until the next spring. So, he worked his way back to Texas as a mere cattle hand.[39]

During the spring of 1886, Saunders again entered the commission business under the firm name of Smith, Oliver, and Saunders, his partners being Frank Oliver of Victoria, Texas, and William Smith of San Antonio. Not long thereafter, Saunders sold his share of the operation to Jace Addington of San Antonio. Saunders then bought and sold all classes of livestock at several locations in that city; by his own accounting, he was "successful in building a good business."[40] He soon associated himself with several other businessmen (many of whom had been trailing contractors) in establishing the Union Stock Yards Company in San Antonio.[41]

Thereafter, as the trailing of livestock northward began to wane in the face of the northern quarantines, Saunders abandoned the transportation phase of the range cattle industry entirely, relying primarily on the cattle commission business for his economic mainstay. About 1900 he incorporated his business under the firm name of the George W. Saunders Live Stock Commission Company, with offices in Fort Worth and San Antonio. By the time of his death, on July 3, 1933, Saunders also owned and operated four small ranches and a seven-hundred-acre farm.[42]

Saunders's investment in a farm, although a relatively minor activity as compared with his other pursuits, is significant because it points up the fact that contractors did occasionally broaden the

70

scope of their financial affairs beyond the restricted limits of cattle-related businesses. Charles Schreiner, for an example, was far better known in Texas business circles for his mercantile establishment at Kerrville than for his major role in the cattle trade.[43] John Lytle and Dillard Fant—although folklore holds that cattlemen and sheepmen hated one another—both also were sheep raisers.

Thomas Jefferson Moore, a Llano, Texas, entrepreneur, is another example of the trend toward conglomerate investment by transportation agents. Born in Tuscaloosa County, Alabama, on March 31, 1847, Moore migrated to Guadalupe County, Texas, with his parents in 1855. At sixteen years of age, he joined the Confederate Army. Following the war, he worked as a teamster and as a drummer. About 1870, he bought a small herd of cattle and drove it northward to Kansas for sale. During the ten years that followed, Moore acquired a ranch in Llano County and invested in the Llano County Bank. By the time the trailing era ended, Moore owned several thousand acres of ranchland, was part owner of the Union Stock Yards Company of San Antonio, and controlled the Llano bank. Indeed, its name soon was changed to the Moore State Bank.[44]

Moore, of course, was not the only transportation agent who found other pursuits to be lucrative. Cattle baron George W. Littlefield, who had once been active in the trailing business, became as well known throughout the Southwest as a banker (through his total control of the American National Bank of Austin) as he was as a cattleman. Contractor John Henry Stephens, as a final example of the conglomerate tendency, became one of the more important real estate agents of the Middle West and Southwest. He was even engaged by the XIT Ranch to sell its southern Yellow House Division to cattleman-banker Littlefield.[45]

Transportation agents, as a group, were a varied lot. Each firm (and every individual) operated in its (and his) own way. Horizontal, vertical, or conglomerate, each sought to make money —even if it were necessary to produce a wild west show in order to sell livestock. They improvised; they innovated. In all probability, their enterprising spirit could be attributed to their youthfulness. Of the twenty-two major contractors discussed herein, the oldest was fifty-four when the postwar trailing era opened in

71

1866; the youngest was twelve.[46] Their average age at the outset of the period was 27.22 years.

Contracting was a physically demanding occupation, and youthfulness for a transportation agent was an advantage—if not an absolute necessity. Had they been generally older, their eagerness to experiment with business techniques and investments might well have been tempered by the caution of middle ages. But, at best, such an explanation can be applied only to some of the contractors, for even in the generalization they defy effective analysis.

At the End of the Trail: Marketing

6

TO WIDE-EYED, six-year-old Helen Lytle, reared in a staunchly conservative Catholic enclave in South Texas and accompanying her father northward to Kansas railhead-markets, Dodge City was a continuous din of excitement. While she and her older brother, George, observed cowboys loose on the town—behaving in a manner they would never have attempted at home—her father sought buyers for the tens of thousands of cattle his firm annually trailed to market.[1] And there were scores of dealers ready to do business with the transportation agent. Dapper men in city dress representing stockyard companies, commission merchants, and meat packers in Kansas City, St. Louis, and Chicago poked at steers to estimate their worth, discussed prevailing market prices with trailing contractors, and wired home offices for instructions. Railhead-markets during the trail-driving season teemed with economic activity as buyer and seller met at the end of the trail. It was there that supply first confronted demand.

In that confrontation at Abilene, a dozen years before, marketing methods were established, and even though that city eventually was supplanted as the center of the cattle trade, the procedures originally employed there were altered remarkably little. The scene in Abilene in 1867 was that of Dodge City in 1880. The characters and the settings changed, but the technique of supply meeting demand was as predictable as the unchanging way transportation agents moved cattle to market.

Joseph G. McCoy's novel idea—"to establish a market whereat the southern drover [contractor] and the northern buyer would meet"[2]—is yet another example of American entrepreneurial genius. Altruistic it was not. McCoy was promised liberal compensation, a percentage of the freighting business, by the

73

Kansas Pacific Railroad should his project prove successful. His commission amounted to $2.50 per carload of livestock shipped eastward each season from his pens, and it constituted his economic mainstay. Moreover, the businessman supplemented his income through buying, fattening, and selling to eastern speculators and packers as many Texas Longhorns as he could afford to handle.[3]

But McCoy was not the only cattle buyer with whom Texans could trade. Representatives of cattle commission companies descended upon Kansas railhead-markets early each spring. These men and their diverse firms aided sellers to locate buyers, receiving for their trouble a percentage of the sale; they also purchased trail livestock for speculative purposes, not infrequently fattening animals they acquired and ultimately selling them either to stock raisers who sought to expand their herds or, more commonly, to meat packers who slaughtered the beeves, dressed the carcasses, and distributed the meat regionally and nationally. Too, there were the employees of stockyard companies in Kansas City, St. Louis, and Chicago who advised cattlemen to ship their animals to their respective cities to await sale, hopefully at a more substantial price. This was the basic scenario.

Typical of the businessmen who capitalized upon McCoy's bonanza were those who located at Kansas City. The driving force behind the establishment of the stockyards there was L. V. Morse, then superintendent of the Hannibal and St. Joseph Railroad. Morse correctly theorized that thousands of western-raised cattle, shipped eastward by contractors unable to sell at the Kansas railheads, would be marketed at the first available place. That could be Kansas City. In 1870, railroader Morse, acting for the Hannibal line, acquired five acres of land near the confluence of the Kaw and Missouri rivers. He had the site fenced, eleven stock pens built, fifteen loading ramps erected, and two Fairbanks scales, to avoid the necessity of guesswork in cattle weight, installed. The railroad then incorporated the operation as the Kansas City Stock Yards Company and offered stock in it to the public. Its management, with J. M. Walker of Chicago as president, was officially organized in March, 1871—just in time to send agents westward to greet early trail herds from Texas. Within the year, the Kansas City Stock Yards Company acquired and improved an adjacent twenty-one-acre tract. That year it processed

120,827 cattle, 41,036 hogs, 4,527 sheep, and 809 horses. By then, every railroad that passed through Kansas City had built its own spur to the facility.[4]

During the fifteen years that followed, the Kansas City Stock Yards Company grew apace, as did the national trade in livestock. The firm's physical plant expanded continuously over the period. In the spring of 1872, the company erected an exchange building to house its offices and those of commission agents doing business in Kansas City. Three years later the structure had to be expanded to accommodate additional tenants. In 1887, new quarters, containing one hundred offices, were built and the old facilities razed. Meanwhile, the stockyards had grown. By 1876 the operation sprawled over some one hundred acres of land along the east bank of the Kaw River. Six 60,000-pound scales had been installed, sheds built in which to store feed for the animals, and elevated walkways erected for the convenience of prospective cattle buyers. In 1886, the company acquired land across the Kaw River and built on it segregated facilities for Southwestern livestock, lest Texas fever destroy domestic animals quartered at the yards. All told, by the end of the cattle-trailing era, the operation represented a half-million-dollar investment in the livestock trade.[5] But the clearest indicator of business activity at the Kansas City Stock Yards was the growth of its cattle receipts:

1871	120,827	1881	285,863
1872	236,802	1882	439,671
1873	227,680	1883	460,780
1874	207,088	1884	533,526
1875	174,754	1885	506,627
1876	183,378	1886	490,971
1877	215,786	1887	669,224
1878	175,344	1888	1,056,086
1879	211,415	1889	1,220,343
1880	244,709	1890	1,472,229[6]

And it was on the volume of livestock traffic that the Stock Yards Company depended for its profits. Joseph G. McCoy observed:

As soon as a train bringing stock arrives at the [Kansas City] yards and is drawn up to the platform for unloading, the employees of the yard company (and there are many) at once open the doors and put down a small bridge from the car floor to the platform, and drive the stock out and down the inclining platform into the alleys, along which they are hastily driven to a yard [a pen] of adequate size, into which they are turned. Soon after, they are watered and fed according to order of shipper. Large barns for storing baled hay and corn are provided, and a shipper can have his stock fed either or both, and only has to pay for the amount he orders; and if no sale of his stock is made, no charge is made for yardage [use of stockyard facilities] or reloading, which is done by the stock yard company. Only in case of sale are charges of yardage made for stock, which includes weighing.[7]

Additional revenues for the yards arose from fees charged railroads for yard privileges (as seen previously in the case of McCoy at Abilene) and rent collected from commission agents who leased offices at the yards.[8]

The commission companies in turn profited from trading livestock. Much like the trailing contractor, the commission agent was a middleman:

The business of the live stock commission merchant is to take care of, feed, water, sell, and render to the owner an account of such consignments of live stock. . . . It is part of his duties to keep himself fully posted as to prices, not only in the market in which he sells, but of all distant markets, besides always keeping a sharp lookout for live stock buyers of all grades; and, in short, to keep and be a kind of general intelligence office concerning live stock men and matters.[9]

Caring for the livestock was merely a responsibility these entrepreneurs readily assumed in order to further their actual business activity—the selling of animals—and to receive a commission on the transaction. Most of them operated on a cost-plus basis, i.e., they charged the owner of the cattle for all expenses incident to the livestock's maintenance, plus a fee for locating a buyer and consummating the sale. The agent's commission usually ranged from 5 to 10 percent of the total sale price of the cattle.[10]

Numerous enterprising individuals, soon after the establishment of the stockyards at Kansas City, located there to capitalize upon the lucrative business. The first commission company to begin operating at the yards was Gilman Reed & Company, which opened an office adjacent to the facilities in March, 1871; in the spring of 1872, it relocated in the exchange building. By then there were seven different commission agencies vying for business at Kansas City. Ten years later, there were more than fifty such firms.[11]

W. A. Rogers, a partner in the Chicago-based commission house of Strahorn & Company and who later was characterized by Joseph McCoy as one of the most substantial and successful of all the agents, in 1871 decided to open a branch office at the new Kansas City facility. At first operating under the name of Strahorn & Company, Rogers began building a business in Kansas City. By the end of the year, his firm had sold for clients almost 2,000 carloads of livestock. The following year, the Kansas City branch office's name was changed to Rogers, Powers & Company —even though Rogers continued his interest in the Strahorn Commission house. Over the ensuing twenty years, Rogers, Powers & Company processed an estimated 100,000 carloads of cattle, hogs, and horses.[12]

Another early cattle trader in the Missouri River city was Joseph L. Mitchener. Born and reared in Pennsylvania, Mitchener early was exposed by his father to cattle-feeding operations. About 1837 the youth moved to Cincinnati where he bought and sold livestock. Twelve years later, he opened in the city a small meat-packing plant, which he operated for five years. Then, heeding a longing to return to rural surroundings, in 1854 Mitchener moved his family to Warren County, Illinois, where he established a stock farm on 700 acres of land. Five years later, Mitchener again moved, this time to St. Joseph, Missouri, where he was associated with a meat-processing firm. He remained there until the Civil War compelled him to remove his family northward to the relative safety of Chicago where, in 1864, he became a division superintendent of the Union Stock Yard and Transit Company. Shortly thereafter, he appointed his son and future business partner, J. Parker Mitchener, weighmaster for the yards. In 1869 the Mitcheners resigned and established in the city the commission house of J. L. Mitchener and Company.

Three years later, they moved their operation to Kansas City, where they soon developed one of the community's leading trading agencies.[13]

Some merchants at Kansas City specialized. J. L. Mitchener apparently did little but buy and sell cattle; others, such as John T. and Charles Sparks, dealt exclusively with horses and mules. Born in Saline County, Missouri, in 1858 and 1861, respectively, John and Charles Sparks were reared on a farm, where their father occasionally traded draft animals to supplement the family's income. At the age of fifteen, John moved to Marshall, Missouri, and associated himself with an older brother in the operation of a stable. By the time Charles joined his brothers in the business in 1879, they were selling horses and mules at the livery. Soon thereafter, John and Charles left Marshall for Kansas City, where they established the Sparks Brothers Company and began plying their specialized trade at the stockyards. Like most of their competitors, the Sparkses disposed of many of their animals to the government, which required horses for the cavalry and mules for pack animals. By 1885, their volume apparently exceeded 20,000 head of livestock annually.[14]

But the larger commission houses traded all types of livestock, for profits were to be extracted from a wide variety of transactions. The firm organized and directed by Robert D. Hunter is a classic example of the business diversification that could be categorized under the general term "commission agency" and of the business acumen that these entrepreneurs frequently displayed.

Robert D. Hunter, born in Ayrshire, Scotland, on April 3, 1833, migrated with his parents to Bunker Hill, Illinois, nine years later. There, the young Scot grew to manhood on the Hunter farm and received what has been described as a "fair education." In 1858, he married Janet Webster of Bunker Hill and briefly settled down to farming. A year later, however, exciting stories of gold discoveries at Pikes Peak titillated his imagination, and, with a group of friends, he joined the fifty-niner movement to Colorado. Hunter panned for gold at Russell's Gulch but was only moderately successful. The following year, he moved to Arizona and prospected in the Superstition Mountains; however, hostile Apaches forced him to return to Colorado later that year. Locating in the remote San Juan Valley in the southwestern corner of the state, he again searched for commercially exploitable deposits of mineral wealth. About 1861, he discovered a rich quartz vein, which promised to lead to gold. Thwarted in his efforts to develop the inaccessible property, however, Hunter rejoined his family, which by then had moved to Denver. There, perhaps because of the rigors of his past four years of wandering and exposure, he collapsed. He was bedridden for almost a year.[15]

Recuperated, Hunter moved his family about 1864 to southern Missouri. He again entered business, this time forming a company to supply oxen to freighting firms that hauled goods to nearby Kansas. Two years later, Hunter saw the same conditions that Southwestern cattlemen observed: the North required meat, and Texas had millions of cheap, marketable cattle to fill the demand. He reached the same basic conclusion as had Texans: drive the animals to Missouri railroads for sale at a substantial profit. Leaving home in the spring of that year, he rode horseback southwestward toward Texas. In the Indian Territory he met a small trail herd of 400 Longhorns en route to Sedalia. The Missouri businessman immediately bought the cattle for $10,000, hired the crew, and ordered the drovers to proceed on to the railhead. In Vernon County, along the southwestern border of Missouri, the sheriff halted the drive, as the Longhorns were suspected of carrying Texas fever, and arrested Hunter.[16]

Obviously anxious lest his entire capital investment be lost, Hunter concocted a scheme to free himself and his livestock. After surreptitiously instructing his trail boss to flee with the herd at the first opportunity, the businessman then suggested that the sheriff take him to Lamar, Missouri, the county seat, where "friends could be found to go his bail." The officer agreed, and the two departed. Not long thereafter, Hunter's crew rapidly drove the cattle westward some thirty miles to the Indian neutral lands, out of the grasp of Missouri law. Upon arriving in nearby Lamar, Hunter offered to buy the lawman a drink in the first available saloon, to dissipate the afternoon's heat, and the sheriff readily agreed. The nervous entrepreneur readily supplied the money, the lawman the thirst. After several hours, the stupefied sheriff lay "blubbering and wallowing in the street." Hunter, assuming he had posted sufficient bond, mounted his horse, rode westward, and rejoined his men. Without further difficulty, the cattle were driven northward through Kansas and then eastward to Bartlett Station, Missouri, on the Rock Island Railroad, where they were sold. After expenses, Hunter cleared $6,000.[17]

The entrepreneur's first experience with contracting, dangerous though it had been, convinced him that the cattle trade then offered the best opportunity for profits. In 1867, Hunter bought 1,200 Longhorns in Texas and drove them to Omaha, where he profitably sold them to businessmen supplying Indian Reservations. If he engaged in the trade at all the following year, evidence of such activity has not been uncovered. But in 1869, it is known that he returned to Texas, acquired title to 2,500 cattle, and drove them northward for sale. Apparently unable to find a suitable buyer, he shipped them to Chicago. Again, his contemporaries assert he profited, even after the freighting expenses were deducted. The next year he cleared a phenomenal $28,000 on the transportation and sale of 1,400 Longhorns.[18]

In 1871, Hunter became a major contractor—only to sustain heavy losses. He bought 5,000 Texas cattle that year and trailed them to Kansas. After they were sold, the drovers paid their wages, and other expenses incident to the drive tallied, he had lost several thousand dollars. It was then that the entrepreneur abandoned contracting entirely. Hired in 1872 by the Kansas Pacific Railroad to drum up business among cattle shippers, Hunter moved to Ellsworth, Kansas. While there he began a limited sideline activity, trading in cattle; by the fall of 1873, he was a substantial commission merchant, aiding drovers to dispose of trail herds and buyers of all types to acquire suitable livestock.[19]

Having decided that larger profits and safer investment opportunities rested with buying and selling livestock at the major stockyards, Hunter in 1873 severed his relations with the railroad, closed his Ellsworth commission house, and moved to the new Kansas City stockyards. By then, that facility was receiving annually more than 250,000 head of cattle. There he happened upon Albert G. Evans, founder and co-owner of Patterson, Evans & Company, a commission house recently established in the city. Evans's partner was eager to sell his share of the operation, and Hunter purchased his half. The house of Hunter, Evans & Company was born. It soon became one of the largest commission concerns in the nation.[20]

Evans's background was remarkably similar to that of Hunter's. Born in Evansville, Arkansas, in 1832, Albert G. Evans remained in the small community, which his father had founded, until 1849 when, stricken with gold fever, he joined the epidemic of prospectors surging westward to California. For four years he panned for wealth in the gold fields of that state, acquiring sufficient funds by 1853 to return eastward. Settling in Gonzales, Texas, he opened a mercantile store and bought a small, nearby ranch where he raised a few head of cattle. In the summer of 1862, he was recruited by firebrand secessionist Thomas N. Waul as quartermaster for the 2,000-man Waul Legion, then being organized to fight in the Civil War. Shortly thereafter, Evans was advanced to captain, a rank he held throughout the conflict. Following his parole in 1865, he returned to Gonzales and resumed management of his mercantile store, this time taking on a partner, W. D. W. Peck. As specie was in desperately short supply in Texas immediately after the war, Evans and Peck accepted livestock in payment for goods. By 1869, the businessmen had sufficient cattle for a trail drive, and they sent several thousand head of Longhorns to Abilene for sale. In the three years that followed, the two dispatched additional drives northward. So lucrative was the activity that Evans decided to devote himself exclusively to the cattle trade. In 1872, he sold his Texas holdings to Peck, moved his family to Kansas City, and joined in partnership with Edward W. Patterson (sometimes written as Pattison), an Indiana cattle buyer who previously had operated a meat-packing plant in the city. That year, the men organized the commission house of Patterson, Evans & Company at the Kansas City stockyards. The following year, Hunter arrived in the city just in time to buy out Patterson, who was eager to return to Indiana.[21]

Evans and Hunter made a curious pair. Evans was once described as "one of those noble-souled men who loves humanity at large and never refuses to aid any known worthy object or enterprise presented to him that has for its purpose the betterment of any one or more of the human race."[22] Hunter, on the other hand, was a cold, calculating example of Social Darwinistic entrepreneurship. Once, when criticized for his predatory business methods, he retorted, "I will run my business or run it to hell."[23] His employees considered him a "hard man." Both they and his business rivals feared him. Hunter once testified under oath, "About the 10th or 12th of June I recollect having an interview in my office with Lawson [an employee] in which I gave him a very severe cussing. Lawson did not insult me on that occasion. I just voluntarily gave him a cussing."[24] Working together, Evans and Hunter became millionaires.

In 1874, Hunter, Evans & Company opened a branch office in East St. Louis, Illinois, at the National Stock Yards. The firm also hired agents to travel westward to Kansas railhead-markets to offer Texans who were unable to locate buyers there the services of their company. In 1877, a second office was located at Fort Worth, with F. W. Flato, Jr., of Austin as resident agent and manager. Then, that year, the partners closed the Kansas City house, designating St. Louis as their home office. From there and Fort Worth they continued to send agents about the country-side to ferret out business for their firm.[25]

In all probability the decision to transfer most company operations to the St. Louis area was prompted by the partners' need to supervise more closely other interests there. When the concern had opened its branch in East St. Louis, it had simultaneously invested substantially in the National Stock Yards Company. Moreover, in 1876, Hunter, Evans & Company opened a beef-canning plant, with a daily capacity of 500 head of cattle, in the Mississippi River city. This profitable sideline continued until 1879 when a fire gutted the facility. Rebuilt in 1880 at a cost of $250,000, the new plant had twice the output of the previous one. A few months later, the partners sold the meat cannery to eastern investors. About five years later, Hunter and Evans reopened their branch office in Kansas City, with M. D. Scruggs, a former partner in the St. Louis commission house of Scruggs and Cassidy, as manager. When Scruggs resigned in 1887, Evans moved from St. Louis to Kansas City and assumed management of that office.[26]

The growing concern also acquired land and raised its own livestock. In 1876, it reportedly leased pastures in Kansas and Nebraska on which it placed feeder cattle purchased by its agents at railheads. Sometime later, Hunter, Evans & Company bought acreage near El Paso and on the Dry Fork of the Missouri River in Montana, where it placed stocker animals. About 1881, the firm leased 432,000 acres of Cheyenne and Arapaho land in the Indian Territory. By 1885, it grazed 16,000 head of livestock on the latter tract; all told, it pastured 60,000 cattle. It was in August of that year President Grover Cleveland, concerned both with cattlemen illegally placing their herds on Indian land and with huge livestock syndicates, such as Hunter, Evans & Company, leasing tribal property at ridiculously low rates, ordered all the cattlemen to vacate. Hunter, Evans & Company had little choice but to move its herds to other pastures, thereby crowding its ranges and threatening all its animals with starvation.[27]

By then, Hunter was reportedly disgusted with the cattle trade. The trails were being closed by quarantines, and company agents could no longer buy Texas slaughter beeves as cheaply as before. The government's action relative to the Indian Territory made stock raising much more costly, for the firm now had to locate other pastures—frequently paying substantially higher lease fees. So, Hunter offered to sell his half of the concern to Evans, but the Arkansan was unable to raise sufficient capital to buy one-half of what was one of the largest commission houses in the United States. Finally, in 1888, Hunter agreed to surrender his share of the operation to several investors—including Evans, M. P. Buel, A. J. Snider, and F. W. Flato—for a figure somewhat in excess of $500,000. By the time of this transaction, which resulted in the organization of the Evans, Snider & Buel Commission Company, Inc., Hunter's firm all told had bought and sold approximately 700,000 cattle, 800,000 hogs, and 350,000 sheep. Adding its former meat-canning operation and its stock-raising activities to its commission business, the company's gross annual revenues easily had averaged more than $500,000 during the previous decade.[28]

While the new Evans, Snider & Buel Commission Company expanded operations, by opening a branch office in Chicago, Hunter moved to Texas. With his son-in-law, Edgard L. Marston, he again became a miner. The Johnson Coal Mining Company, operating in Palo Pinto and Erath counties, just west of Fort Worth, was beset by a crippling strike. W. W. Johnson, president of the floundering firm, in May, 1888, readily accepted Hunter's offer to buy 8,888 shares in his company, the controlling interest. The St. Louis businessman then moved to Fort Worth and organized the Texas & Pacific Coal Company (so-named because the Texas and Pacific Railroad served the mines and was the coal company's largest customer), with himself as president and Marston as treasurer. The new chief executive's solution to the labor strife, precipitated by the miners' demand for higher wages, was to lock out the workers and import strikebreakers. Within nine months, partly because a company of Texas Rangers was called in to maintain order and to protect Hunter, the strike was broken. The miners were forced to accept an even lower scale of wages, their alternative being unemployment. Thereafter, Hunter ruled his company-owned town of Thurber as a feudal lord. In 1889, he resigned the presidency in favor of his son-in-law and retired to Fort Worth. He died there on November 8, 1902.[29]

Entrepreneurs such as Robert D. Hunter were not alone in capitalizing upon the livestock trade, fed by the Texas cattle trails, which developed at Kansas City. Meat packers were also attracted. Edward W. Patterson, later a partner of Albert G. Evans in a Kansas City commission house, in 1868—even before the Kansas City Stock Yards Company was established—founded E. W. Patterson & Company in the city. Patterson, who previously had operated plants in Indiana and Kansas, soon took on an associate, J. W. L. Slavens of Kansas City, who similarly had engaged in the commission business. They erected on the Kansas side of the Missouri River a stone building with a daily processing capacity of 250 cattle and 1,000 hogs. The following year, Slavens withdrew from the concern, selling his share of the firm to Dr. F. B. Nofsinger of Indianapolis; soon thereafter, Nofsinger acquired Patterson's half of the business and leased the plant to the Plankinton & Armour Company of Milwaukee. By then there were three meat-packing plants operating in the city.[30]

Slavens had reentered the field in 1869 and associated himself with Indiana meat-packer J. C. Furgason to form J. C. Furgason & Company. A plant, which daily dressed 500 cattle and 1,500 hogs, was erected near the Plankinton & Armour operation. The following year, J. H. Mansur of Boston moved to Kansas City and began processing hogs. These two companies were moderately successful, but their ownership changed so frequently over the ensuing decade that one might easily infer that their owners were more eager to speculate than to process meat.[31]

The same charge may not be leveled at two other meat-packing plants that located in Kansas City during the trail-driving era. First and foremost was the Plankinton & Armour Packing Company, founded in Milwaukee in 1863 by John Plankinton and Philip D. Armour. By 1870, when these businessmen opened

84

facilities in Kansas City, they operated branches in Chicago and New York. The following year, the company bought land in Kansas just south of the point at which the Kaw joins the Missouri River and erected on it a massive two-story building. That year the Kansas City plant processed 14,000 cattle and 30,000 hogs. In 1873, its physical size was doubled and an ice plant and chill-room added. By 1876, the operation in Kansas City—by then enlarged again—worked 600 persons and paid annual wages of $110,000. By 1891, employment had risen to 3,400 people and the annual payroll to $1,250,000.[32]

Second in importance at Kansas City was the plant owned by George Fowler, Son & Company. Organized originally as the Anglo-American Packing Company, it opened a meat-processing facility in the city in 1880. Four years later, George Fowler, an executive of the company, acquired sole ownership of the concern and immediately expanded its physical plant. By 1886, George Fowler, Son & Company was processing annually 10,000 cattle and 425,000 hogs. At the end of the decade, the company employed 1,000 workers and paid annual wages of $360,000. By then, its sales each year exceeded $6,000,000.[33]

By the end of the cattle-trailing era, other major meat packers similarly had opened plants in the city. In 1880, the Jacob Dold Company of Buffalo began operations on the Missouri River. The James Morrison Company of Cincinnati in 1884 acquired facilities near the Stock Yards Company. Three years later, Swift and Company of Chicago built a plant near the Morrison Company. Also that year, Kingan & Company, Ltd., of Indianapolis and Belfast, Ireland, opened a branch nearby. Kansas City, by seeking to funnel western-raised livestock to itself, became a leading center for the meat-packing industry.[34]

Similar trends of urban and economic development during the period occurred at Chicago and St. Louis. The national demand for foodstuff and the almost endless supply of slaughter beeves from the West and Southwest finally met in these cities. The vacuum that originally existed between supply and demand in 1866—and which enterprising Texans eagerly sought to fill—was also capitalized upon by equally adaptive entrepreneurs at the end of the cattle trails. The stockyard companies provided the marketplace where commission agents brought buyer and seller together. And ultimately, in the final confrontation between

85

supply and demand, the slaughterhouses transformed bawling beeves into sides of meat—meat that eventually fed the nation.

The Economic Impact of Trailing 7

BUCK WINTERS, a cowboy who was driving cattle from Texas to Dodge City, awoke one morning, checked his pockets, and discovered that he was broke. He related this bit of news to one of his companions, who immediately reminded Winters that he had had $50 only the night before. Then Winters, scratching his head, began to clear the cobwebs from his mind. He recalled his night in the nearby town during which he had visited three saloons and bought drinks around for everyone there at a cost of $10 or $15 per round. His friend accurately noted that Winters had accounted for merely $35 of the $50. Winters unabashedly concluded, "I uz gettin' pretty drunk. I'm afraid I must have spent the other fifteen dollars foolishly."[1]

On such foolish spending, many a frontier trail town based its economy. The sharp report of a pistol shot, the shattering crash of breaking glass, the rowdy noise from saloons where tired and dusty drovers drank cheap whiskey and conversed with loose women about Longhorn cattle (and other subjects not so delicate), although far from characteristic of a stable society, constituted good evidence that the village was thriving economically. Should the nights become peaceful, then the community stood in financial peril. Since each cattle herd sold on the northern market funneled hard currency into the towns along the cattle trails, as well as into the area from whence it came, trail traffic created a fluid economy for many frontier villages.

Blessed with a product that could transport itself to market, cattlemen nevertheless found a sizable investment necessary to

Portions of this chapter appeared as "The Economic Impact of Trailing: One Aspect," West Texas Historical Association *Year Book*, XLIII (October, 1967), 18–30, and are reproduced herein through the courtesy of the Association.

trail a given herd northward. Ranchers used a rule of thumb for estimating cost: about sixty cents per head for every 1,500 miles traveled. A federal government study in 1886 estimated the cost at about seventy-five cents per head,[2] while the XIT Ranch itemized its expenses, less the initial cost of the livestock, for a 2,000-head drive during the 1880s at:

wages	$1,340.00
chuck bill	386.27
watering expenses	48.00
other	27.23
total	$1,801.50[3]

Of this amount, only the $386.27 food bill was disbursed primarily, but not entirely, at the point of origin. The drover was paid his salary, less what he had borrowed against it, upon reaching the railhead-market. Watering and "other" expenses (which included the frequent charges made by Indians for allowing cattlemen to graze their trail herds on the reservation) were contracted along the way. Thus, of the total cost of a drive, about 80 percent was spent in an area north of the point of origin.

Two obvious and well-known recipients of the economic benefits of the cattle-trailing industry were, first, the railroads, which transported the beeves on the last leg of their journey to midwestern slaughterhouses and, second, the cities in which those packing houses were located. Railroads seldom publicized their rate of profits from the cattle trade, but available evidence indicates that returns were impressive. The Kansas Pacific Railway Company, for example, published "for gratuitous distribution" five separate editions of its *Guide Map of the Texas Cattle Trail* (1871–1875), which encouraged drovers to follow the Chisholm Trail to company stock pens in Kansas. Ellis, Russell, Ellsworth, Brookville, Salina, Solomon, and Abilene were advertised by the *Guide Map* to offer the best facilities for the transfer of livestock to rail shipment. And by 1874, as evidence of its expertise and prowess, the Kansas Pacific Railroad claimed to have hauled all told no less than 923,749 head of Texas Longhorns—or substantially more than 40 percent of all the traffic. Appended was a detailed log of the Chisholm Trail, giving distances, landmarks, river crossings, and supply points between the Red River crossing and the railroad's shipping points in Kansas. For those who would have difficulty following a verbal guide, a detailed map was included.[4]

Packing houses at such points as Kansas City and Chicago processed the animals offered by cattlemen for foodstuff. In 1870, only 838 people in Missouri and Illinois were employed by the packers; ten years later, the combined figure has skyrocketed to 11,960. For Chicago, according to urban historian Bessie Louise Pierce, the meat-packing industry was a substantial factor in the city's economic and metropolitan growth.[5]

But the most dramatic effect of trailing was not national; it was local. It enabled otherwise unstable frontier communities to survive. The impact of cattle drives upon Abilene, Ellsworth, Wichita, and Dodge City, Kansas, is not only obvious but well documented.[6] Not so well known, however, are the stories of the isolated frontier villages that served as supply points and prospered along the paths of the cattle trails.

A trail town existing far west on the frontier, away from the stabilizing influences of farmers, frequently found it absolutely necessary to cater to the delights of the cowboys. Joseph G. McCoy, observer of many of the wildest trail towns, characterized such settlements as "sin holes":

> And with them [gamblers] are always found their counterparts in the opposite sex; those who have fallen low —alas, how low! They, too, are found in the frontier cattle town; and that institution known in the West as the dance house [the bordello], is there found also. When the darkness of night is come to shroud their orgies from public gaze, there miserable beings gather into the hall of the dance house, and "trip the fantastic toe" to wretched music, ground out of dilapidated instruments by beings fully as degraded as the most vile. In[to] this vortex of dissipation the average cow-boy plunges with great delight. Few more wild, reckless scenes of abandon and debauchery can be seen on the civilized earth, than the dance house in full blast in one of the many frontier [cattle] towns.[7]

Since cowboys tended to spend their money wherever they happened to be, it is not difficult to understand why bitter rivalries occasionally developed between towns for the lucrative trail business. In 1872, rather than see drovers stop off in Fort Worth and use the new facilities of the Texas and Pacific Railroad, the city fathers of Denison, Texas, encouraged Missouri, Kansas and Texas Railroad officials to offer $100-per-carload rates. Such ploys were largely fruitless, for most Texans continued to trail their herds to Kansas, from which rates averaged only $30.[8]

Fort Worth promoters also recognized the potentially enormous profits of the cattle trade. Merchants reaped handsome returns from the drovers who paraded through town, but, for some, this was not enough. In 1875, an editorial worthy of any booster organization appeared in the Fort Worth *Democrat*: "There is no reason why Fort Worth should not become the great cattle center of Texas, where both buyer and seller meet for the transaction of an immense business in Texas beef. Fort Worth promises every advantage required in doing a very heavy beef packing business. With an abundance of pure water, ample herding grounds and soon to have shipping facilities by rail to all the markets of the East and North, it would seem an admirable point for packing beef."[9] But the appeal for a packing plant for Fort Worth, at least for the time being, fell on deaf ears.

And too, within a few years, the problem of the cattle trade for Fort Worth and other communities along the Chisholm Trail had changed dramatically. In 1876, better than 300,000 cattle were driven to market in Kansas, and the following year's volume was almost as large. But by 1877 two separate cattle trails existed —the Chisholm Trail, through east-central Texas, and the Western Trail, which had been blazed by transportation agent John Lytle along the ninety-ninth meridian. In order to capitalize upon drovers' spending, vigorous communities along both routes sought a lion's share of the traffic. One of the more intriguing skirmishes developed in 1877 between Fort Griffin and Belton in Texas. Merchants from Fort Griffin sent advance agents beyond Belton to encourage contractors to turn west and take advantage of a relatively farmer-free route, thereby, of course, visiting Fort Griffin. Belton retaliated with similar tactics and even enlisted the aid of Fort Worth businessmen who undoubtedly would benefit if drovers followed the Chisholm Trail through their city. Three-fourths of all trail traffic that year remained on the Chisholm Trail, notwithstanding the efforts of enterprising Fort Griffin promotors; but thereafter, the majority of the herds turned west, for the Western Trail to Dodge City—as advertised—was better suited by 1878 to the cattle trade.[10]

To secure the drovers' business, trail-town saloons, not unlike the communities themselves, often went to extraordinary lengths. Women of easy virtue, as cowboy J. L. McCaleb once noted, were common in cattle towns such as Abilene. McCaleb once entered a bar there, and one of the girls came up to him and, he said, "put her little hand under my chin, and looked me square in the face and said, 'Oh, you pretty Texas boy, give me a drink.' " McCaleb eagerly complied with the request and, arm-in-arm with the woman, set out to break the saloon's bank by playing monte. Both his money ($9.00) and his female companion soon had vanished. The situation in Wichita, to the south, was little different. By 1872, four organized bordellos operated openly in the city. Conditions in an unincorporated suburb just across the Arkansas River were even more riotous, but prostitution figures for West Wichita are unavailable. Apparently no one visited the community merely to count.[11]

A decline in drovers' spending could be disastrous for a community with a trail-oriented economy. Abilene, for an example, had been one of the earliest and mose prosperous of all the Kansas railheads. Joseph McCoy reported that in 1867 Texas money had transformed it almost overnight from a sleepy, farming hamlet into a boisterous, active city. Profits, however, failed to compensate citizens for the outright bawdy and otherwise questionable characters who soon located in the community. In 1870, barely three years after it had first seen trail herds driven down its main thoroughfare, the City of Abilene enacted stringent vice laws, closing all the brothels and forcing the prostitutes out of town. Immediately, drovers found ample reason to drive their herds elsewhere, receipts of the Abilene stockyards the next year diminishing by a full 15 percent and community revenues falling appreciably. City fathers, anxious lest the local economy be entirely wrecked, reportedly allocated tax money to buy forty acres of land south of the city and to build on them "the Devil's addition to Abilene," replete with liquor, women, and gambling.[12]

The situation in Abilene had grown so bad by the end of the season of 1871 that several local groups were diligently seeking to evict the cattlemen in order to cleanse the city of sin and degradation. The newspaper leaped on the bandwagon and advised drovers not to return with their herds in 1872. Newton, Kansas, recently reached by the Atchison, Topeka, and Santa Fe Railroad, however, was eager to have the business; therefore, in 1872, because of encouragement from Newton, and in order to get away from the hated sodbusters of Abilene, cattlemen abandoned that railhead. By the spring of 1873, four-fifths of the business establishments in Abilene were vacant, and, by midsummer, petitions begging the Texans to return were widely circulated among the townspeople. Unfortunately for the city, the damage already had been done.[13]

Such privations were not unique to Abilene. Dodge City, the last of Kansas's rip-roaring cattle towns, almost died in 1885 when the state's legislature quarantined all cattle capable of commuicating Texas fever—i.e., the majority of trail traffic. Many Dodge City businessmen (owners of such well-known enterprises as the Alamo, the Comique, the Lady Gay, and the Long Branch saloons) quickly picked up and moved west of Trail City, Colorado, which was not then subject to quarantine laws.[14]

While trailing continued, however, frontier communities prospered. Coleman, Texas, located on the Western Trail, had been settled in 1876, the first year that any discernible volume of traffic followed that route northward to Dodge City. While herds watered in Hords Creek, then slightly more than a mile north of town, drovers imbibed stronger draughts in the local bars. By the end of the first year of trail traffic, no less than three saloons were operating in the tiny village. A race track even was opened near the town to afford additional amusement for the drovers and, doubtless, to extract additional revenues from the cowboys.[15]

Readily aware of the economic importance of trailing, townspeople organized to promote it and even dispatched riders toward the south every day from the first of April until late fall to greet trail bosses and to invite them to linger in Coleman. Such measures apparently paid high dividends, for the town boomed. Almost all businesses either directly or indirectly were related to the cattle trade. By 1880, on both sides of its hundred-foot-wide main street (broadened to handle a herd of cattle passing through town), a countless variety of establishments (including a dozen saloons) offered their wares. At night, reportedly the only women seen were prostitutes. Even the community's cemetery is said to have received its first resident after one cowboy shot another. Coleman's population grew rapidly and, apparently, in relation to trail traffic. In 1860, Coleman County reported no residents; in 1870, it recorded 347; ten years later—and before farmers in any significant number had settled in the county—there were 3,603 inhabitants.[16]

The Flat at Fort Griffin is yet another example of a community with a trail-oriented economy. Organized in 1867 as a crude collection of clapboard buildings near the new military post, the Flat capitalized upon soldiers, buffalo hunters, and drovers—in that order. When the buffalo trade was about exhausted (or about the time Fort Griffin merchants were trying to divert cattle drives from Belton), the town became an important supply base for trail herds that plodded the Western Trail. At first, about 1874 when Indian raids presented a very real danger, contractors heading toward unstable Indian country had routed their herds through the community to secure military escorts. Following the successful Red River Campaign of 1874–1875 (when the immediate threat of Indian depredation was removed), cattlemen continued to trail Longhorns past the fort because the neighboring village catered to their needs and delights. As there was no official law and order in the town—other than that occasionally administered by the military—the Flat soon acquired a reputation for bawdiness, rivaling even that of Deadwood and Dodge City. Charlie Meyers, owner of the Bee Hive Saloon, did a thriving business in what he boasted was the "best and wildest tavern west of Fort Worth." As proof of his assertion, he claimed that it was a rare week when his place of business was not shot up by at least one drunken drover.[17]

Carefree cowboys were not alone in starting trouble at the Flat. Myers and the other saloon operators hired trollops to entertain drovers, the most famous of whom were two known as Millie McCabe and Lottie Deno. Local authorities (at first the vigilantes and later a deputy sheriff from the county seat at Albany) seldom brought charges against either the women or the procurers. Community leaders were fully aware that their town's economy rested substantially upon the drovers' business, which was largely enticed into the Flat by widespread prostitution. The first of each year the women were hauled into court and charged with running a disorderly house; a plea of guilty was followed by a standard

93

fine ($100). They were not arrested again until the first of the following year when, once again, a formal complaint would be lodged against them. The system amounted to a method of licensing the brothels. Indeed, one observer was doubtless correct when he asserted, "Not only were these women permitted to run their houses by paying fines, but when they committed other offenses it was very difficult to find a jury that would convict them."[18]

Because of the general lawlessness, a vigilance committee was organized about 1878, but it was designed to keep disorder within reason, not to cleanse the community completely—an action that doubtless would have ended the town's appeal to the cattle trade.[19] The group, however, could dispense swift justice. Once when Frank Collinson, a drover turned buffalo-hunter was camped with another hunter (Jim White) on the Clear Fork of the Brazos River, not far from Fort Griffin, a posse from the Flat rode pell-mell into their camp and demanded whether or not White knew one of the men they held captive. Had the startled frontiersman not correctly identified the man as George Causey, another buffalo hunter, the posse, according to Collinson, would have hanged "him to a tree . . . with some horse thieves who had been found in his camp."[20] Collinson, however, had no grievance against the vigilantes or the Flat. After all, the saloons in the community had not been closed. Only drastic action such as that would have constituted a grave injustice to the cowboys, for, as Collinson once observed, "water is primarily intended to wash in and [to] mix with things more drinkable."[21]

Oregon City, as Seymour, Texas, was known in 1878, likewise saw the absolute advantages of maintaining amicable relations with the countless, thirsty drovers who paraded through town from early spring until late fall. In 1880, a two-story hotel was constructed there to capitalize upon trail traffic and upon westward-moving migrants who traveled through town on an east-west immigrant road. According to A. P. Black, a drover who often visited in Seymour, the trail town was well aware of the economic importance of the trail. He even claimed that city fathers erected a two-story courthouse to prevent irate and drunken cowboys riding through town on horseback from shooting the judge. Whether or not the new courthouse was designed to decrease the mortality rate of local judges, as Black insisted,

Seymour did grow beside the trail. In 1890, the community reported 1,125 residents, an increase of almost ten times over the preceding census figure.[22]

Even very late in the century, when trail-driving was little more than a short march to Tascosa or Amarillo, the situation had not changed appreciably. Ella's Dance Hall, as Amarillo's most famous bordello was euphemistically known, was the chief source of entertainment for the cowboys, drovers, cattlemen, and local residents. Indeed, clients of Ella Hill's establishment were most respectful of the madam. Her personal lawyer was the county attorney, and she not infrequently lent considerable sums of money to some of the more important and powerful merchants and ranchers in the area.[23]

Albany, Texas, strategically located at that point on the Western Trail where the Potter-Bacon Trail splintered northwestwardly to traverse the Texas Panhandle, offers perhaps the best single example of what trail traffic could mean to a frontier village. Although the townsite was platted in 1875, it was not until 1876—when there were herds in sufficient numbers to support an economy—that the first business, a general store, was established. By 1880, the population of Shackelford County had climbed to 2,037, of whom 980 lived in Albany. One year later the county's population had jumped to an estimated 5,000. Tax assessments, one of the best indicators of economic growth, had likewise risen; the county in 1881 listed the worth of taxable real estate as $755,262, more than double the total of the previous year. The tax base continued to climb until 1885 when, at the peak of trailing, it temporarily stabilized at $2,367,821. Civic leaders accurately credited trail traffic as being the mainstay of the obviously phenomenal growth.[24]

One of the many businesses that sought earnestly to capitalize upon Albany's prosperity was the firm of Webb, Campbell, and Hill. The enterprise was organized as a land and cattle company in 1886, when the firm of Campbell and Hill merged with that of Webb and Webb.[25] L. W. Campbell, a lawyer and later general counsel for the Texas Central Railroad, and Louis Hamilton Hill, a land agent, had used their respective talents to profit from the real estate boom, which since 1880 had been characteristic of Albany; W. G. and Sam Webb, father and son, respectively, had been active in the cattle trade for several years.[26] The combined organization thus hoped to profit not only from the source of Albany's growth but also from the community's anticipated future.

Unfortunately for the Webb, Campbell, and Hill Land and Cattle Company, 1886 was not an outstanding year for the cattle-trailing industry. First and foremost, by the end of 1885, Arizona, Colorado, Kansas, Montana, Nebraska, New Mexico, Wyoming, and even Canada had enacted legislation seriously restricting the importation of all cattle capable of carrying Texas fever. These actions had been taken to prevent the total destruction of the northern range cattle industry, a calamity that, by then, seemed imminent to many northern ranchers.[27] Only those cattle bred in and trailed from South Texas actually were capable of communicating the disease, but the net result of the various quarantines was to stifle trailing. As already shown, one of the largest Texas transportation agencies, Lytle, McDaniel, Schreiner, and Light, was literally destroyed by these pieces of restrictive legislation. In 1884, Lytle's concern handled 91,000 head of livestock; in 1887, it moved only 12,000. The company was dissolved that year. Moreover, by 1885, farmers had migrated in large numbers into West Texas, thereby, of course, limiting the cattleman's freedom of movement while on the trail. Barbed wire had been strung across the trail at some points. And local railroad facilities by then allowed ranchers to ship directly, albeit more expensively, to northern processing centers. In 1885, trailing was on the wane.

This, then, was the economic climate in which the Albany firm of Webb, Campbell, and Hill began its operations. The first effects of the quarantine were felt in Albany in early January, 1886. Sam Webb confided to veteran cattleman C. C. Slaughter that, since his community fell north of the actual quarantined area, cattle prices for locally raised livestock should remain high. Thus, Webb added, area ranchers were "*dubious*—actually afraid to put a price upon them [their cattle], unless it is a very high price." Webb seriously doubted that the market would support needlessly inflated prices.[28]

Indeed, few cattlemen knew fully what to expect from the quarantines. Webb, Campbell, and Hill, obviously eager to keep abreast of the situation, advised one correspondent:

> We had a long "consultation" with two of our largest and most substantial cattlemen to-day, and they were

96

both at *sea* as to what they would do—both prefer[r]ing to deliver at home. One agreed to deliver 2000 N. W. Texas raised 2 year old steers (nearly all raised in this County) in Fall River Co[unty], Dakota, for $19.00, and at Dodge (if the quarantine would admit [them]) for $18.00. You are no doubt aware that Kansas is very strict with her quarantine laws, and while they have generally admitted cattle from this County and section, she may at any time refuse to do so; hence you will not find one in five hundred [trailing contractors] who will agree to deliver in Kansas.[29]

And although Shackelford County ranchers anticipated high prices for their cattle, the firm noted that "buyers here expect a low market."[30] As the concern advised one prospective seller, "We have to say that we do not think we could use any two year old steers if you were to offer them delivered at Albany for $8.00. The bottom has completely dropped out of [Texas] cattle, [and] *we are sick!*"[31] Some cattlemen, such as rancher-contractor George West, even considered abandoning cattle entirely and turning to sheep.[32]

With the cattle trade severely weakened, the partners began to worry about the prospects of their business. Campbell had so little faith in the firm's future that he elected not to remain with the company. He left in 1888 for Waco and became an executive with the Texas Central Railroad. Meanwhile, the communities along the moribund Western Trail, suffering an intense depression because of the precipitous decline in cattle trailing, had banded together in hope of establishing the Cattle Kings' (or Cattle Trail) Railroad, which would run northward from Coleman to the Santa Fe Railroad at Dodge City—or essentially the route of the Western Trail. Webb and Hill vigorously supported the proposed line; a map of the projected path was even added to the firm's letterhead. Bickering over the precise right-of-way, due in part to the desire of Abilene, Texas—not on the cattle trail—to have the road pass through its city limits, however, doomed the project to failure. As Webb in 1889 advised Campbell, his former partner, "Now in regard to the Cattle Kings' R. R., we are afraid it is a R. R. on paper."[33]

The full impact of this depression in Albany is best seen in one of the sales attempted by Webb, Campbell, and Hill. Late in 1886 the firm had been engaged to sell the Barnes House, a two-story hotel in the city. They dutifully advised a prospective buyer in Dallas, George W. Hyreson, that the hotel contained more than a thousand dollars' worth of furniture, twenty-four sleeping rooms (eight of which were double rooms), a cottage on the grounds for the proprietor, a cistern for drinking water, a fire-proof safe in the office, and a good clientele comprised primarily of cattlemen en route to Dodge City. They further noted that the boom-town rent of $132.40 per month on the building recently had been scaled down to $100 per month "until times get better." Moreover, the business, easily worth $3,500, was being sacrificed by the owner "because of his health" for $3,000. The major selling point was that "Albany is on the old 'Cattle Trail' you hear so much about."[34] Hyreson soon retorted, "I have learned from a gentleman who has a ranch only 1 or 1½ miles from your town that place is dead and has been for over a year."[35] Notwithstanding the Albany firm's protest that "the gentleman [had] lied,"[36] Hyreson refused to buy. More than six months later the hotel was still on the market, its owner's asking price having shrunk to $2,800. The rent on the building likewise had been lowered—to $75 per month. In their letters to advertise the property, no longer did the agents dwell upon the importance of the cattle trail or upon the cattlemen en route to Dodge City who once patronized the establishment.[37]

By August, 1887, life in Albany was so dull that the business-men began to boast of their community's lawful character, a far cry from the conditions in the frontier trail town of three years earlier. The concern claimed in a sales pitch aimed at a Kentucky resident interested in moving to West Texas that there was not "a single saloon in the County," and that murders were rare. It was even asserted that "there is *far less lawlessness in Texas than there is in Kentucky,* [for] . . . there are no feuds in Texas."[38] Business was so curtailed, however, that rumors of Albany's becoming a ghost town were widely circulated. Sam Webb de-nounced the charge: "We beg to call your attention to the fact that this town is not *dead,* but will soon wake up and have such an era of prosperity as has seldom been witnessed in any County."[39] But the partners could not escape the basic fact that the business climate in Albany was *"very dull, and while we hope for a bright future, [we] can not say when it will come."*[40]

All aspects of the real estate business in Albany reflected the soft economic conditions that had prevailed once trailing had begun to decline. Rent houses in 1887 were available for as little as $4 to $6 per month, with few takers. Webb, Campbell, and Hill advised one client, "There are so many vacant houses that it is impossible to get any tenant to take a house for *love* or *money.*"[41] In 1888, even though a serious drought had abated, the situation had not improved. Land prices and rent levels were even lower than they had been the year before.[42] By 1890, the firm of Webb and Hill had almost totally abandoned trading in livestock.[43]

As for Albany, the rosy picture of 1885 had wilted. In 1890, after the trail was but a fading memory, for all practical purposes, the county's population had declined to 2,012, not only fewer persons than the 5,000 people estimated in 1881 but well below the 1880 census figure, also. It was not until 1930 that Shackleford County reported a population greater than the 1881 estimate.[44]

Numerous factors, such as the drought of 1886–1887, the transition of the cattle trade from the wheeler-dealer aspects of the open-range era to the more conservative business practices of planned management, and so forth, affected the economic climate of all the frontier communities that served as trail towns. Even so, it appears obvious that the loss of trail traffic constituted a grave crisis. It is significant to note that every frontier village that suffered a recession during the period did so simultaneously with the decline of trailing. With a little less luck—and certainly without the farmers who moved westward—it seems all of these isolated communities could have suffered a much more severe fate and become ghost towns of the American West.

It is obvious that the transportation phase of the range cattle industry tremendously influenced town growth along the frontier of Texas and at the Kansas railheads; similarly, the railroads that shipped beeves to slaughterhouses and the cities in which those meat-packing plants were located also gained economically. It is equally clear that enterprising Texans—the John Lytles, the Eugene Milletts, the Ike Pryors—established personal fortunes by trailing livestock to northern markets. Even the ranchers who engaged transportation agents to drive their herds northward benefited; if the case of the Matador Land and Cattle Company may be considered typical, then trailing cut the rancher's transportation cost in half, alternatives being exorbitantly expensive direct rail shipment from Texas or diversion of ranch employees to time-consuming, costly drives.[45]

But it apparently was not so obvious to those improvising, innovating entrepreneurs—the contractors—that their unique business ploy was shortsighted economically. In 1870, Texas contained more than a dozen slaughterhouses, butchers and packers grossing in sales $1,500,000 annually. A mere decade later the trailing of cattle northward had become so ingrained in the Texans' business tradition that the state processed only about one-third as much meat.[46] Yet, the national demand for foodstuff had increased. Ranchers and contractors by then simply were conditioned by conventional practice to market their animals outside the state. By doing so, both the cattlemen and the region lost financially. Had the enterprising genius and dash that contractors originally demonstrated been channeled into establishing large meat-packing companies in Texas, into organizing feasible transportation facilities to ship their finished product to market, and into encouraging retail outlets to merchandise their meat, their profits—and their significance in history—would have been far greater. The ranchers' transportation costs easily would have been reduced even more; hence, their profits also would have increased. But even more importantly, the economic impact of the ranch and range cattle industry in the West and Southwest would have been multiplied enormously.

In essence, Texas and the rest of the cattle-producing West and Southwest served the East as a colonial outpost in a mercantile framework. Cattlemen supplied raw material that was processed further eastward, and the overwhelming majority of profits in the meat industry came from the "value added" by processing. Thousands more Westerners could have worked for nationally important meat packers located in the area than ever were gainfully employed by cattle contractors. Therefore, even though the transportation agent was important to the region—by providing jobs for drovers, by performing a service for ranchers, and by furnishing a fluid economic base for frontier cattle towns —his activities also had a countervailing impact. With him the area benefited economically; conceivably, with him as a meat

100

packer, it would have prospered immensely. Millions of dollars flowed into the West and Southwest during the three decades following the American Civil War because of the rancher and the contractor; hundreds of millions more would have flooded westward had the meat-packing industry been centered there. Fort Worth might have surpassed Chicago's record in the trade, and Denver that of Kansas City.

The National Trail Issue and the Decline of Trailing

8

NO EVENT—not the stringing of barbed wire, not the relentless westward movement of farmers, not droughts nor blizzards —played a more fundamental role in bringing the trailing era to a close than did the several northern quarantines of the middle 1880s. The problem was that Texas Longhorns, carriers of Texas (Spanish or splenic) fever, left death and destruction in their wake wherever they were trailed, and by 1884 northern stockmen were vocally demanding that the importation of the disease-carrying cattle cease. Texas cattlemen, especially transportation agents and ranchers who operated in the southern half of the state, immediately set out to thwart any state restrictions on the movement of their livestock by securing for their animals a federal highway, a thoroughfare that would not be subject to local prohibitions and would guarantee trailing's continuation. Thus, the National Trail issue began.

The quarantine movement was not new in the 1880s, for Texas fever had long ravaged northern herds. As early as the eighteenth century, it had been suspected that some Texas cattle were infected with a peculiar pestilence; but with the exception of some scattered quarantine measures in a few states during the 1850s, little serious concern was attached to the malady until the mass movement of South Texas Longhorns began, following the Civil War. During the 1850s, as a few foresighted Texans began

Portions of this chapter originally appeared as "The National Trail Issue and the Decline of Trailing," *Museum Journal*, XI (1969), 1–24, and are reproduced herein through the courtesy of the West Texas Museum Association.

to drive their surplus animals northward for sale, northern stock raisers began losing large numbers of livestock to the disease. In Missouri in 1854, several thousand cattle reportedly died after being exposed to Longhorns. The Missouri legislature's reaction to the destruction of its domestic livestock was to enact a law in 1855 that prohibited the importation of "diseased cattle." A $20 per head fine doubtlessly discouraged many from driving herds into that state the following year. Similar outbreaks of Texas fever in Kansas in 1858 led its territorial legislature to pass a measure not unlike that of the Missouri statute.[1]

But the situation did not improve. Two years later, faced with yet another fever scare, Missouri strengthened her ordinance against Texas cattle by empowering county inspectors to destroy suspect animals, if necessary. Only the intervening Civil War prevented an actual test of this quarantine measure. Kansas also, in 1861, tightened her prohibition against diseased livestock by outlawing the importation of all Texas cattle between April and November.[2]

Soon, hard economic reality led in 1866 to a revision of the Kansas law. Without qualification, the state threw open its borders to any and all trail herds,[3] doubtlessly recognizing that the mass movement of Texas cattle thereby could be funneled to its railroads—particularly to the pens that Joseph McCoy was then preparing at Abilene. Thus, Kansas began welcoming the great trail drives of the postwar period.

As a steadily increasing number of Texas Longhorns were trailed northward after the Civil War, Texas fever predictably reappeared. In 1866, a Chicago firm purchased forty thousand Longhorns fresh off the Sedalia Trail and pastured them with a large herd of domestic animals. The Texas cattle gained weight and stamina, but the domestics inexplicably began to die. Simultaneously, Shorthorn cattle in Kansas, previously exposed to Texas animals, sickened and died. South Texas livestock, having become immune to the disease, were unaffected, while northern Shorthorns died in an estimated ninety-nine cases out of a hundred.[4]

The symptoms of Texas fever were unmistakable. One observer said:

> [An] elevated temperature exists for from four to six
> days before any other symptom [in the cattle] can be

104

observed. There is a dullness, want of appetite; in cows, a diminished secretion of milk; pulse quick and weak, generally ninety to one hundred; quick, panting respiration. As the disease advances, the urine is dark-colored or bloody—this is a very characteristic symptom; the breath has a fetid odor, and there is evidence of great nervous prostration, the animals staggering on being made to move. Delirium and lethargy are also frequent in latter stages of the disease. Those affected with delirium throw their heads about violently, and sometimes in doing so fracture their horns. Cows or oxen affected with coma will remain in one position, and it is only by main force that they can be made to move.[5]

Almost everyone associated with the range cattle industry, it seems, postulated a theory as to Texas fever's cause. One individual concluded that it resulted from dormant spores peculiar to Texas grasses: when the grass was eaten by Longhorns, the microbes entered the bloodstream, where they multiplied and afterward infected all short-horned cattle that came into contact with the carriers. This hypothesis, however, failed to explain why the Longhorns did not likewise die. A second theory maintained that the disease was the result of the long drives northward: Texas livestock received inadequate food, water, and rest while on the trail, thus weakening their innate resistance to illness; the fever, therefore, was a "scurvy-like" malady that infected native cattle whenever they came into contact with the carriers. This explanation also failed to clear up the mystery surrounding the Longhorns' healthy appearance and to show, as scurvy is not communicable, how the disease was transferred to the northern animals. As late as 1883 seemingly sophisticated government and lay observers charged that the soil of the Texas Gulf Coast was contaminated with a "poison," which was transported northward by Longhorns supposedly immune to the toxin. Eventually it was more correctly assumed that Texas fever was caused by cattle ticks (*Boophilus bovis*) indigenous to Southwest Texas. After centuries of exposure to the organisms, Longhorns had become immune. Proponents of the tick theory pointed out that the fever always ended after these parasites had been destroyed by a killing frost.[6] Even the tick answer was later proved inadequate.

Although records fail to disclose the exact number of live-stock destroyed by Texas fever, the matter was serious. In 1906, Dr. John R. Mohler, chief of the Pathological Division of the Bureau of Animal Industry, estimated that between 1866 and 1889 (essentially the trailing era), cattle valued at $63,000,000 were lost to the ravages of the disease.[7]

And almost without exception, quarantine measures passed during the early years of trailing were ineffective—if not totally circumvented. The Illinois legislature's attempt in 1868 to protect its domestic livestock industry seemed adequate, for the law expressly forbade any importation of Texas cattle. Before the measure could be applied, Joseph G. McCoy of the Abilene Stock Yards, doubtless in alliance with Chicago meat packers, quickly brought pressure to bear on the lawmakers. Soon, an amendment to allow the importation of Longhorns that had been wintered in Kansas was passed. Thereafter, all herds shipped from McCoy's pens, not surprisingly, were accompanied by documented proof that they had been "wintered" at Abilene.[8]

Cattle raised in North Texas were even susceptible to the fever. By 1880, a great proliferation of cattle trails resulted in South Texas animals being trailed across the Panhandle-Plains of Texas and, predictably, the transient herds left fever epidemics behind. In July, 1880, Panhandle cattlemen, meeting at Mobeetie, Texas, firmly resolved to close the Potter-Bacon Trail through their territory by designating two alternative routes around their pastures. They even went to the added expense of building stock tanks at regular intervals so that trail drivers could not complain about a lack of water and, consequently, have some justification to cross the closed *Llano Estacado* ranges. But when, the follow-ing year, South Texans ignored the request and again used the Potter-Bacon Trail, the Panhandle stockmen—led by Charles Goodnight, who had seen 975 of his own cattle die from the disease that year—once again met at Mobeetie and drafted a letter to Governor Oran M. Roberts demanding a quarantine against South Texas livestock. But this and similar appeals to the legislature went unanswered, for South Texas lawmakers (who outnumbered legislators from the Panhandle-Plains) held firm for their constituents. Having failed in their attempt to secure legal protection, the Panhandle ranchers wrote a letter to the Fort Griffin *Echo* and sent copies to transportation agents who plied

106

the *Llano Estacado* route, warning them against using the Potter-Bacon Trail in 1882. Goodnight and his neighbors then posted armed men at the edge of the Caprock, in case any trail boss ignored the blunt warning of the "Winchester Quarantine."[9]

Farther north, cattlemen were becoming desperate. In 1884, some 5,000 South Texas cattle were trailed through Wyoming. Within a few weeks of the herd's passage, an avalanche of letters inundated the headquarters of the Wyoming Stock Growers' Association; each detailed the wholesale destruction of livestock from Texas fever. Some ranchers lost a hundred head daily, while reports of thirty head were not uncommon. Without effective quarantine laws, northern cattlemen were legally powerless to stop the trailing of disease-carrying South Texas livestock through the open range. De facto measures, however, grew on the precedent set by the Texas Panhandle-Plains cattlemen. In the Oklahome Panhandle, stockmen erected barbed-wire barricades on government land, until the military forced their removal. In Kansas, ranchers marked with furrows on either side a half-mile-wide trail from the southern boundary of their state to the railhead at Dodge City. Outriders were posted, carbines in hand, ready to shoot any cattle that strayed from this narrow path. Meanwhile, another group of southern Kansas cattlemen organized and sent forth a manifesto to South Texans telling them to take their herds elsewhere, and many reportedly took the advice and went west to Colorado rather than risk an open confrontation.[10]

Kansas ranchers, although acting outside the precise letter of the law, were demonstrating the long-standing official attitude of their state. In 1867, Kansas, wishing to protect its domestic livestock industry without losing the revenue it derived from trail herds, had amended its 1866 statute, which had thrown open that state's doors to Texas cattle, by placing a quarantine line through Kansas along the sixth principal meridian, or 97°22′. Thus, South Texas cattle could be trailed legally to points such as Ellsworth, Wellington, and Wichita. By 1872, the Kansas cattle industry, like the population of the state, had shifted westward, and a new line was drawn from Wichita westward along the Arkansas River to the southwest corner of Rice County (due east of Great Bend), and back eastward to the original line. More than half of Kansas was still open for use by disease-carrying Longhorns. Four years later, the line was altered to protect livestock east of Ford County

107

(Dodge City). Two further changes in the law, in 1877 and in 1879, inched the line westward, but Dodge City remained a legal railhead.[11]

Thus, Kansas was faced with a dilemma it hesitated to resolve. If it quarantined the entire state, it would lose Texas money. On the other hand, if it allowed Texas trail herds to continue using its rail facilities, it could incur major financial losses through the destruction of its own livestock industry. But since 1867, the populace of Kansas had grown increasingly weary of Texas fever losses. The laws that had been passed were not effectively enforced, as stock raisers of Detroit, Kansas, angrily pointed out.[12] Early quarantine measures were ineffective, perhaps, because officials, such as Dickinson County (Abilene) Sheriff H. H. Hawlett, readily aware of economic realities, denied that Texas fever posed any real danger.[13] But as time passed and as losses mounted, outcries of protest from financially injured Kansans poured into the state capital demanding that existing laws be enforced and, occasionally, that they be significantly expanded.[14] Indeed, Governor G. W. Glick in August, 1884, by executive order quarantined the entire state for the remainder of the trailing season.[15] And by then the Kansas legislature was ready to translate Glick's action into firm law—a fact soon generally known throughout the range cattle industry.

South Texans were understandably worried about the situation. If Kansas completely closed its borders to their trail herds, cattlemen would be forced to drive their livestock farther westward, through Colorado, to reach northern railheads and ranges; moreover, other states, such as Colorado, might follow suit and enact similar legislation. Even though railroads had been available in Texas since shortly after the Civil War, Texas ranchers had haughtily shunned their services because of the lower cost involved in hiring a transportation agent and patronizing the northern rail lines, which offered cheaper rates. But if South Texans were forced to add more miles to trailing, their overhead would increase and profits would diminish; if the trails were totally blocked, they claimed they would face disaster.[16]

With this black cloud over their heads, South Texans began to look forward to the fall of 1884. A call had gone out the previous January for the cattle industry to organize nationally, and a meeting for that purpose was to be held in St. Louis the following autumn. The entire beef-producing industry was to be represented in the convention—the first of its kind.[17] Soon rumors were being circulated that the South Texans would use the convention to secure relief from the threatened quarantines. Colonel B. B. Groom, general manager of the Panhandle-based Francklyn Land and Cattle Company, early in November advised his company's secretary in New York, Frank G. Brown, that it would be advantageous for Groom himself to attend the St. Louis meeting. According to the general manager, South Texans planned to ask the convention to adopt a National Trail resolution. They wished to see the federal government create and maintain a cattle trail northward from Texas, for federal control (as it overrode state law) seemingly would guarantee trailing's continuation. Three routes, according to Groom, had been widely discussed among Texans. One would cross the Red River at Doan's crossing on the Western Trail and then turn northwestward to pass through Mobeetie in the Texas Panhandle, eastern Colorado, and Wyoming to Canada. Another would depart from San Antonio and strike a new route northwestward to Clarendon in the Panhandle, angle back northeastward through Dodge City, and then continue northward to the Canadian border. The last—and the one supported by Groom because it did not bisect any of the Francklyn's ranges—would follow the Western Trail northward from San Antonio, cross the Red River at Doan's Store, veer northwestward to the 100th meridian (or the eastern boundary of the Texas Panhandle), and follow that line to Canada.[18]

Similar to Colonel Groom's concern and apprehension over the St. Louis meeting was that expressed by other Texas Panhandle-Plains stockmen. William F. Sommerville, boss of Matador's Texas ranching operations, wrote his superior:

> As I have received no further orders to proceed to the ranch I presume the order is not insisted on & I shall therefore go to St. Louis to attend the convention. It seems to me important someone should represent this Co[mpany] there as matters of vital interest to us will come up, particularly the question of the quarantines or prohibitions of Texas cattle by Northern States & in this connection, the definition of the Panhandle [as being fever-free] & of a "trail" for Southern cattle. [I] shall do what I can.[19]

Rumors of the South Texans' plan were widely circulated even outside Texas. By January, 1884, the Ford County *Globe*, speaking on behalf of directly affected Dodge City, and somewhat broaching the South Texans' case, was openly calling for the passage of a federal highway act to guarantee an outlet to the Kansas railroads and northern ranges.[20] In April, 1884, the Stock Growers' Association of Western Kansas almost destroyed itself in a riot when Dodge City-led proponents of trailing further insisted that the path to Dodge remain open. The majority, however, demanded that the association call upon the state legislature for a comprehensive quarantine law and that the group oppose any attempt by the Texans to secure relief through a National Trail scheme. One of these cattlemen, after stating that some people were interested only in Texas money, concluded:

> [H]ow can it be expected that, with our countless thousands of high grade cattle, we should continue to permit the passage of hundreds of thousands of through Texas cattle annually in our tracts, through the heart of our grazing country, leaving germs of disease which have already cost stockmen hundreds of thousands of dollars from losses incurred, without any compensation or direct benefit whatever[?] We are convinced that the time has now come when this should cease.[21]

Northern cattlemen, enraged over the massive losses they had suffered, were ready to fight.

When on November 17, 1884, the national cattleman's convention finally opened, Texans descended upon St. Louis in full force. Twenty-one states and territories sent delegates, but Texans comprised 47 percent of the total. Moreover, many of the "Northern" delegations, such as the twenty-seven men representing the Kansas City Stock Yards, for obvious reasons were openly sympathetic to the South Texans' cause. From the very beginning, the convention was destined to be a Texas-dominated show.[22]

About 9 A.M., the stockmen began arriving at the St. Louis convention hall. Some feeble attempts had been made to decorate the place for the visiting cattlemen. Two bouquets of flowers in "cow horn vases" had been placed on the speaker's rostrum and, below, on the platform, cacti and sprigs of northern pine—perhaps an attempt at sectional balance—added touches of color.

110

Shortly before the session began, several dignitaries took their seats on stage. Mayor E. A. Ewing of St. Louis was eager to welcome the delegates to his city; Governor Thomas T. Crittendon of Missouri had a long roll of paper from which he would soon address the gathering; and General William Tecumseh Sherman added glamour to the setting. Twenty-five hundred delegates, wives, and interested spectators were jammed into the hall when, promptly at 11 A.M., St. Louis commission agent Robert D. Hunter rapped with his "cow horn gavel" and called the convention to order. The long-awaited session had finally begun.[23]

Following preliminary orations of welcome, the first item on the agenda concerned committee representation. How would representation be determined: by individual associations, by states, or how? Judge W. T. Thornton of Santa Fe, New Mexico, insisted that the final apportionment reflect states, separate associations, and total capital invested in the cattle trade—or an extension of the relative delegate strength already prevailing. Opposition was immediately voiced by those cattlemen whose state and association delegations were not as large as those of Texas, Kansas, and Colorado. General W. M. Curtis of New York, the sole representative of his state, dismissed the matter as trivial and insisted it be settled by giving equal voting strength to all the states. Immediately, L. R. Rhodes of Denver vaulted angrily from his seat, demanded and received the floor, and proceeded to tell Curtis why the dispute was none of his business. Rhodes asked Curtis if he knew the difference between the National Trail and a public highway; even if he did, Rhodes contended, it would not matter, for the National Trail issue concerned the West and not New York. The delegate from Colorado concluded by proclaiming that his state was entitled to the committee representation that her capital investment and delegate strength demanded. Moreover, he added, she would have it. The temporary chairman, C. C. Rainwater, rather than see the convention erupt at that moment into a free-for-all, hurriedly called for a vote on representation. The convention approved a method of allotting committee assignments through separate, member associations—a system which decidedly favored the larger states with several livestock organizations. Rainwater then quickly adjourned the morning session.[24]

When the cattlemen began to arrive at the convention hall

111

for the afternoon meeting, which was to begin at three, the conversations naturally turned to the National Trail. Henry Milne, a member of the Lincoln County (New Mexico) Cattlemen's Association, probably expressed the views of many of the delegates when he confided to a journalist that the National Trail presented northern stockmen with a dilemma. Most ranchers justifiably feared Texas fever, Milne admitted, for if the disease continued to spread it could destroy the entire northern industry. Nevertheless, he insisted that a National Trail would have certain advantages, even for northern ranchers. For one thing, it would force Texans to confine themselves to one route, thereby lessening the chances of contact between Texas cattle and northern animals. Milne also shrewdly noted, "I think it [a National Trail] practicable, and the chief need of it is to serve as a check on the railroads. The existence of it will prevent them from charging exorbitant rates."[25]

Nevertheless, a large portion of the convention remained resolutely opposed to the National Trail; in order to secure its passage, South Texans found a quid pro quo necessary. Many northern cattlemen favored a resolution which would call on Congress to provide for the leasing of huge blocks of land, thereby withdrawing large chunks of the open range from the public domain and from immediate use by the homesteader. South Texans, unaffected by the measure inasmuch as Texas had retained her public lands when she entered the Union, agreed to support the leasing measure in return for the passage of the National Trail resolution. The proposal on leasing soon passed by a voice vote.[26]

The National Trail resolution was then introduced by Joseph G. McCoy, the founder of the Abilene Stock Yards and the man who had done as much as anyone to bring Texas trail herds to his state. With the support South Texans had gained by vote-trading added to that they already had from interested cattle buyers, from those who wished to see Texas cattle restricted to one route, and from those who wished to hedge on railroad freight rates, the motion carried easily by a voice vote. It called on Congress, "in the interest of cheaper food," to establish a National Trail from the Red River boundary of Texas northward to the Canadian border (no specific route was suggested), all necessary lands being provided by the federal government. Texans, especially the eleven major trailing contractors present and the ranchers who were most threatened by proposed quarantines, were elated.[27]

Notwithstanding the seeming unanimity within the industry, many northern ranchers steadfastly opposed the scheme. Stockmen from Kansas and Colorado spent the remainder of the week trying without success either to repeal or to amend the resolution. Others simply walked out of the convention in protest.[28]

Even some Texans seriously doubted that the resolution would carry much weight. William Sommerville of the Matador Ranch accurately predicted disaster for the South Texans and for the new association:

> The writer attended the convention in St. Louis [for] four days. The resolution to go to the U.S. Senate [sic] with a memorial or an appeal for a "National Trail" passed by a large majority but if the evidence of strong feelings manifested in the meeting are to be trusted, we should judge that this National "Trail" has little chance of being. Kansas will legislate against it & very likely [will] pass laws prohibiting the importation of Texas cattle between [the] 1st [of] May & [the] 1st [of] Nov[ember]. It will therefore rest with the Kansas rather than the U.S. legislature to define the infected limits of Texas. We have good hope that the prohibitions will not apply to the Panhandle or to the counties in which we are. The National Assoc[iation] of Cattlemen is not an accomplished fact we fear. Chicago is very jealous of it & stole a march on it by holding a "National Convention" there before the St. Louis one met at which they appointed delegates to confer with a committee from the St. Louis convention as to the organization of a National Assoc[iation].[29]

Aside from failing to forecast the precise dates of the Kansas quarantine, Sommerville's somber prediction came true.

It soon became apparent that the northern cattlemen would not even give lip-service support to the trail resolution. *The Breeder's Gazette*, a journal which openly reflected the anti-trail bias, soon denounced the St. Louis meeting as a travesty of democracy. On November 27, five days after the convention adjourned, the *Gazette* angrily reported that the session had been

113

corrupted by Texans and by Kansas City cattle buyers. In December, the magazine carried the verbatim statements of D. W. Smith and Thomas Sturgis of Wyoming, both of whom had withdrawn from the St. Louis meeting upon the adoption of the National Trail resolution; they asserted that the convention had been staged solely for the benefit of the stockmen "of the extreme west and southwest." Moreover, they issued a call for ranchers to join with them in the Chicago-based "National Cattle-Growers' Association," which, they insisted, would more accurately reflect the views of the entire industry. A convention would be held in Chicago on the following November 17—exactly one year after the St. Louis meeting.[30]

While some cattlemen sought revenge against South Texans by calling for a new convention and association, others renewed their pressure on their respective state and territorial legislatures for comprehensive quarantine laws. Kansas was the first to act. State Representative W. D. Platt in January, 1885, introduced House Bill 116, "An act for the protection of cattle against Texas, Splenic or Spanish fever."[31] The measure provided that between March 1 and December 1 any person driving into or through any county in Kansas any cattle capable of communicating Texas fever would be guilty of a misdemeanor, punishable by fine ($100 to $2,000) and/or by imprisonment (thirty days to one year) in the county jail. Provisions for civil actions to recover damages were made for Kansas citizens under the law.[32] Lest any South Texan infer the stature was a paper blockade, Kansas Governor John A. Martin in July, 1885, by proclamation reminded various state law-enforcement officials of the quarantine and directed them to initiate proceedings against any trail herd that originated south of the thirty-fourth parallel and traveled into or through the state.[33] By the end of 1885, Arizona, Colorado, Montana, Nebraska, New Mexico, Wyoming, and even Canada had passed and were enforcing similar legislation.[34]

Meanwhile, the predominately northern cattle industry had met at Chicago. The National Cattle-Growers' Association immediately disavowed any connection with the previous St. Louis convention, and its members officially withdrew from the National Cattle Growers' Association of the United States. Not only did the group oppose the National Trail in principle, but it also called upon Congress to enact stronger controls over the migra-

114

tion of diseased animals, so long as federal action did not infringe upon states' rights. It openly denounced any other federal action: "For domestic, indigenous disease . . . the local quarantine must continue to be the only safeguard [against widespread infection]."[35]

Moreover, almost as soon as the first northern quarantines had been passed, some Texas ranchers called upon their own state government to solve the fever threat. The Cattle Raisers Association of Northwest Texas, meeting at Sherman, on March 10, 1885, passed this resolution:

> Resolved that owing to the fact that Kansas and other States north and west of us have enacted quarantine laws which practically prevents Texas cattle from being driven through or into such States on account of what they allege to be splenic or Texas fever in Texas cattle, the effect of which is to make the market for marketable cattle in Texas inaccessible, we do therefore most earnestly request our State Legislature now in session to pass a law authorizing appointment of sanitary commissions . . . [to] suggest such a remedy for the existing evils as they think best.[36]

The association further called on Congress to pass whatever laws were necessary to quarantine disease-carrying cattle but to exercise discretion so that the trails would not be totally blocked.

Notwithstanding the North Texans' request, the Texas governor and legislature refused to budge from a pro–South Texas stand. Governor John Ireland, in his initial message to the Nineteenth Texas Legislature on January 13, 1885, called vaguely for legislation on behalf of transportation agents and southern ranchers: "In view of the fact that nearly all of the States are establishing a quarantine system to guard against the importation of diseased stock, and to prevent possible damage, we should adopt some system to protect *our* stock system [italics added]."[37]

The legislature's reaction was to pass a joint resolution that same month: "Be it resolved by the legislature of the State of Texas, That our Senators and Representatives in Congress are respectfully requested to aid in securing the establishment of a national trail for the outlet of Texas cattle."[38]

Thus, the action was transferred to Washington. On Decem-

115

ber 2, 1885, Texas Senator Richard Coke introduced Senate Bill 721; eighteen days later, Texas Congressman James F. Miller of Gonzales submitted a duplicate of Coke's measure as House Bill 2450. These called for the creation of a National Trail northward from No Man's Land in the Indian Territory to an unspecified point along the northern border of Colorado. The necessary lands were to be taken for ten years from the public domain in Range No. 41, a fractional range about two miles in width running along the eastern boundary of Colorado. Both measures were then referred to their respective commerce committees.[39]

The Senate commerce committee, headed by Samuel J. R. McMillan of Minnesota, immediately requested that the Secretary of the Interior, L. Q. C. Lamar, supply the committee with all the facts relative to the proposed bill. On January 19, 1886, Lamar complied with a five-page report in which he touched on the question of the public domain, the state of the cattle industry, and the need for cheap beef in the North. It concluded: "The bill under consideration is a measure calculated not only to facilitate commerce in the interest of the people of [South] Texas, but as well . . . [will] give the people of all parts of the country food at moderate prices. I believe the bill should be passed."[40] On March 4, the Senate commerce committee reported favorably on its bill, and fifteen days later, the measure, surprisingly, received unanimous passage in the Senate.[41]

In the House, two actions transpired. While the Committee on Commerce considered the merits of the proposal, a House resolution on February 17 requested that the Secretary of the Treasury provide suitable information on range and ranch cattle movement. Two weeks later, a printed, two-hundred-page document, styled as *Report of the Chief of the Bureau of Statistics on Range and Ranch Cattle Traffic*, by Joseph Nimmo,[42] was submitted to the House. All views concerning Texas fever, the quarantines, and the National Trail were included. The analysis, in part, concluded: "The large and flourishing trade which has existed for many years in the sale of young Texas cattle at the North to stock the ranges of Kansas, Colorado, Wyoming, Montana, Dakota, and Nebraska has, in years past, been highly promotive of the range and ranch cattle interests of those States and Territories, as well as of the State of Texas. No sort of governmental restraint could properly be interposed to the continuance of that

116

business. . . ."[43] Others were not so certain. Another government report, for example, pointed up the danger of immense capital losses for northern cattlemen, should trailing continue and Texas fever spread.[44]

Meanwhile, the House commerce committee, chaired by John H. Reagan of Texas, gave the proposed piece of legislation a clean bill of health on March 23. It was not until April 23, however, that the measure made its way to the floor. There Reagan led the fight for passage, and even though the bill received a favorable vote (sixty-nine to twenty-nine), it failed to carry for a lack of a quorum.[45] By then, spring drives were under way, and for all practical purposes the matter was out of congressional hands.

As the quarantines had been legislated, the National Trail issue was dead, and Texas cattle, as a result, immediately declined in market value. Matador Ranch foreman William Sommerville reported to his Dundee, Scotland, superior, "The market for young stock has not been bright at any time this season. The quarantine laws enacted by Kansas, Colorado, & New Mexico made contracting hazardous."[46] The cattleman further explained the economic vise that was squeezing Texas ranchers: northern purchasers, because of the quarantines, were made especially aware of the danger of Texas fever—as though each Texas steer were branded with the admonition *caveat emptor*; those who would buy found so many cattle offered that prices, through the law of supply and demand, declined accordingly.[47]

If the situation was difficult for ranches in North Texas, such as the Matador, it was ruinous for South Texas cattlemen and transportation agents. Contractor-buyer John Henry Stephens advised Sommerville: "You are indeed of the lucky ones to be above the Said 34th [Parallel] named in the Kansas law [*sic*]. We of the South happen to be out of luck thus leaving us to open up new fields of old operations, and our old trailmen feel it forcibly."[48]

Sam Webb, partner in the Webb, Campbell, and Hill Land and Cattle Company of Albany, Texas, advised transportation agent John T. Lytle in January, 1886, that the local market appeared unstable. Webb added, "The quarantine is giving this section a *great boom*, for many people are interested in local cattle as they fall outside the quarantined area."[49] But Webb's

117

forecast proved to be shortsighted, for the value of all Texas cattle tumbled by almost 70 percent during the next year. The stigma of Texas fever, called an "unjust prejudice" by some cattlemen, was now mistakenly associated with all cattle produced in the state.[50]

Lytle probably saw the fallacy in Webb's prediction even before Webb did. In some cases Lytle was even unable to secure his full commission on the livestock he trailed northward; with the market value of Texas cattle on a precipitous decline, he was said to believe that he could "not insist on the full com[mission] on the cattle [which] sold cheap."[51] Indeed, his firm, the Lytle, McDaniel, Schreiner, and Light Cattle Company, as has been seen, was totally destroyed by the quarantines.

The National Trail issue was also disastrous for the Southern-dominated Texas Live Stock Association, the largest and most powerful of all the Texas cattlemen's organizations. Following the St. Louis meeting in 1884, it began a concerted effort to block the northern quarantines and secure passage of the National Trail proposal. It sent representatives to Topeka in an attempt to thwart the passage of the Kansas law; it sent lobbyists to Washington to encourage the adoption of the federal bill. By January, 1886, it had a total indebtedness of $1,340, all of which had been incurred in these fights. The association was in serious trouble, because it had but $64.16 on hand. In order to pay the debt, the chairman of the finance committee suggested drastic action, a special (and an additional) assessment of $5 on each member and a one-third reduction, to $200 per year, in the secretary's salary.[52]

Even more important than the organization's large indebtedness was its near dissolution over the National Trail issue. Texans north of the thirty-second parallel (or about Coleman)—whose cattle were susceptible to Texas fever—strongly opposed the livestock highway proposal and, as in the case of Charles Goodnight and the Panhandle-Plains Cattlemen's Association, often supported quarantines. The Panhandle group in 1885 spent $6,519 in Kansas to insure that when that state passed its prohibition, the law would be effective against South Texans and would not affect the Panhandle stockmen adversely. Other ranchers withdrew from the Texas Live Stock Association rather than give aid to the National Trail scheme; some simply refused to pay their assessments.[53]

Indeed, North Texans even repeated the "Winchester Quarantine." Lipscomb County ranchers kept their men on duty round the clock to turn back suspect cattle. Policing of this type was common each year, until the first frost had ended the current danger.[54] The Spur Ranch let it be known that it would not allow the passage of herds through its pastures. Anyone who would ignore the warning "would be treated as a trespasser, and the owner proceeded against for damages."[55] Cattlemen were advised that the trail now skirted Spur pastures. Ranch hands were instructed to watch trail herds and, if necessary, physically block ranch gates so that force must be used to gain entrance. Ranch manager S. W. Lomax assured Spur employees that such action on the part of trail bosses would result in stern, legal consequences.[56]

One of the more serious confrontations between ranchers and drovers because of Texas fever occurred in Garza County, Texas. In May, 1886, a trail herd under the Odom and Lucket Land and Cattle Company brand appeared at a guarded gate on the southern edge of the Spur Ranch, and the unidentified trail boss demanded ingress and egress through the ranch's land because he claimed the gate in question blocked an official post road. Ranch manager Lomax rejected the drover's assertion, saying that the road was private and that it never had been used —officially or unofficially—to carry the mail. The trail boss ordered a halt to his drive, and Lomax quietly sent a rider to Snyder to solicit a legal ruling from the Scurry County Attorney, Garza then being attached for administrative purposes of that county. Spur Ranch hands stood guard, apparently armed, lest the drovers try to force their way through the range. Finally, word arrived, and Lomax, fortified with a legal opinion, ordered the herdsmen to go around the ranch. His bluff having failed, the trail boss meekly complied.[57]

Indeed, once ranchers on the plains of Texas began to enforce their own quarantines, it was to a drover's advantage to offer some proof that his herd was fever-free—if he wished to be passed through strange pasture. The XIT Ranch required such evidence, and spreads such as the Matador, which needed to cross XIT rangeland, eagerly complied.[58]

And still Texas fever wrought destruction. The editor of the Las Vegas, New Mexico, *Stock Grower* wrote in 1887:

The Texas cow bobs up serenely just at a time when the country was felicitating itself that it was to have a short rest from the plague that roameth in the internal economy of that animal. Nebraska was excited last week by the appearance there of Texas fever which is laying low the herds. Now Missouri takes her hat off to the bovine destroyer and says that the Texas cow has got the drop on her. The Texas live stock editor is expected to drape his eyes at this time and refuse to believe the direful news concerning the habits of his beloved cow when she goes abroad. He will also shout about "free grass" and "quarantines" in order to distract attention. The Texas cow, however, maintains her reputation for being the cause of much unhappiness to those who handle her during the summer months outside the state which produces her.[59]

The final blow to trailing Texas cattle came on July 3, 1889, when the federal government, by order of Secretary of Agriculture J. M. Rusk, quarantined all or parts of fifteen southern states. Shipment of livestock located therein to non-quarantined areas, except for limited slaughter, was expressly forbidden.[60]

Thus, the *Boophilus bovis* contributed measurably to the end of the cattle-trailing era. South Texans, who were forced by the quarantines to discontinue the time-honored practice of driving their herds to northern markets and ranges, began in the late 1880s to patronize their state's railroad facilities, and by so doing they pointed the way for all Texas cattlemen. Within four years of the passage of the Kansas quarantine of 1885, the cattle trails —blocked by law—were a fading memory.

Ironically, the trails were scarcely cold when three important steps toward the control and prevention of the disease were taken. In 1890, scientists of the United States Department of Agriculture proved conclusively that Texas fever was caused by a microscopic parasite to which the cattle tick acted as intermediate host. Once bitten by the ticks, the livestock received the microbes, those animals not immune dying as a result. Three years later, the State of Texas created a Livestock Sanitary Com-

120

mission for the purpose of inspecting cattle shipped through or out of the state; the governor was required by law to cooperate with other states and the federal government to control the spread of Texas fever. Then on August 10, 1897, an indirect but successful attack on the microbes themselves was begun when a practical way to kill the ticks was demonstrated publicly. Dr. Victor A. Norgaard of the Bureau of Animal Industry showed cattlemen gathered in Fort Worth that the ticks died when the cattle were dipped in a cleansing solution, and the threat of Texas fever ended.[61]

Norgaard's solution came twelve years too late for South Texans bent on trailing their herds to market. By then, what had been treeless plains were broken by farmers' plows and fenced by ranchers' barbed wire. And with the end of the trailing era, the unique business service offered cattlemen by transportation agents faded into oblivion.

Between
Supply and Demand 9

IF THERE IS romance associated with the cattle-trailing era, it was created by reminiscing drovers, naïve novelists, and stereotype-prone motion pictures. In reality, the driving of cattle to market was a unique business enterprise developed to fill the economic vacuum between supply and demand; it was sustained by railroad competition and by the drovers' own tradition. For the most part, those individuals associated prominently with the transportation phase of the range cattle industry seldom carried a gun, apparently never shot anyone, and rarely romanticized about their own contribution. They were first and foremost businessmen—in the best tradition of improvising, innovating entrepreneurship.

The major cattle-trailing contractors—John Lytle, Eugene Millett, the Coggin brothers, the Pryor brothers, the Blocker brothers, and half a dozen others—all told were responsible for the movement of three of every four cattle driven to railhead-markets and northern ranges during the period. A host of other businessmen who occasionally engaged in the activity perhaps accounted for half of the remainder. Indeed, not more than 10 to 15 percent of all the traffic consisted of purely ranch cattle moved by the cattlemen who had raised the livestock. The competitive nature of contracting is seen in the fact that no transportation agency controlled more than 15 percent of the total traffic.

Contractors were indeed hip-pocket businessmen, perhaps because, in an industry where the working year lasted merely six months, time literally was money, and the bureaucracy inherent in maintaining offices and resulting records would have constituted an intolerable level of inefficiency. Lytle, for an example, did not even have time to concern himself with employees' high jinks, such as the stealing of cattle along the trail. Millett did not even concern himself with locating a supply of livestock until he first had assessed the current demand. Neither businessman created a body of records detailing his individual deals; neither needed such documentation to function effectively in the trade. This was the situation with virtually all of the transportation agents.

The profit motive naturally led these entrepreneurs to be inventive, until a unique business ploy had been developed. John Lytle found sufficient return merely in transporting cattle to market for the owner. Eugene Millett, although he contracted some animals, purchased the majority of those he drove northward. John Blocker relied entirely on buying livestock, driving them northward, and selling them for a profit. John Stephens both contracted for the delivery of Longhorns and served as a commission agent at the end of the trail. Robert Hunter, after some success as a cattle-trailing contractor, turned his attention to the commission business. George Littlefield abandoned the transportation phase of the range cattle industry, became a substantial rancher, and supplied his former business rivals with trail livestock. Although they all operated differently, they had in common the quest for profits—a quest which led them to fulfill the same essential function.

Much the same is true of the businessmen who operated at the end of the trail—the stockyards promoter, the commission merchant, and the meat packer. They too sought to fill the vacuum between supply and demand. If their business methods and resulting records were more orthodox than those of the contractors, it was merely because they worked at a central location. And although their busiest months corresponded with the trailing season, they also were continuously supplied slaughter animals by local stockmen and by the railroads.

The fluid economic base that transportation agents provided to the frontier, although very significant to the areas involved, was both transitory and myopic. When the era ended, localized depression replaced prosperity along the cattle trails. Had those enterprising contractors become Southwestern meat packers, then the regional boom loosed by the national demand for meat would have been extended well into the twentieth century. But they did not transform themselves. When threatened with the loss of their livelihood because of the quarantine movement of the mid-

124

dle 1880s, their response was to seek federal aid in the form of the National Trail. Two ramifications are evident in their action. First, the contractors by then were so tradition-bound that they were incapable of further adaptive innovation—improvisation of the type they had originally displayed. And second, as have most businessmen throughout the history of the United States, transportation agents saw the federal government as a protector and sustainer of the economy—a paternalistic institution supporting private enterprise, even if regulation was inherent in such action.

Had the quarantine issue never arisen, then barbed wire, or irate farmers, or improved and more reasonably priced rail transportation from the Southwest would eventually have closed the cattle trails. The commercial driving of livestock to market was merely an expedient by which the major entrepreneurs offering a unique service grew wealthy. Yet, as with the blacksmith, the sail rigger, and the iceman, the cattle-trailing contractor was doomed to oblivion by further innovation.

Notes

1
Hip-Pocket Businessmen

1. Wayne Gard, *The Chisholm Trail* (Norman: University of Oklahoma Press, 1954), 12–13.
2. The number of men required for a drive varies with the telling: Edward Everett Dale, *The Range Cattle Industry* (Norman: University of Oklahoma Press, 1930), 46, basing his account on the reminiscences of R. C. Tate, a drover, gives the figure of twelve men per 2,500-head herd; Ike T. Pryor, "The Cost of Moving a Herd to Northern Markets," in J. Marvin Hunter (comp. and ed.), *The Trail Drivers of Texas* (comp. ed.; Nashville: Cokesbury Press, 1925), 367, gives the eleven-man figure used herein. Pryor, a contractor, doubtlessly used a minimum of manpower to maximize profits.
3. S. W. Lomax, [Spur] Ranche (original spelling employed by British owners) to J[ohn] H[enry] Stephens, Kansas City, Missouri, July 8, [188]5, in Letters sent, Spur Ranch Records (Southwest Collection, Texas Tech University, Lubbock); B. B. Groom, Austin, Texas, to [Frank G.] Brown, New York, New York, Feb[ruary] 26, 1885, in "B. B. Groom" File, Francklyn Land and Cattle Company Records (Archives, Panhandle-Plains Historical Museum, Canyon, Texas).
4. W[illiam] F. Sommerville, Headquarters Ranch, to A[lexander] Mackay, Dundee, Scotland, January 23, 1885, in "Dundee A" Correspondence, Matador Land and Cattle Company, Ltd., Records (Southwest Collection, Texas Tech University, Lubbock).
5. H. H. Campbell, Tee Pee City [Motley County], Texas, to Mackay, Dec[ember] 29, 1884, in Headquarters Division, Letters sent, ibid.
6. Gard, *The Chisholm Trail*, 222; [James W. Freeman (ed.)], *Prose and Poetry of the Live Stock Industry of the United States* (Kansas City, Mo.: Hudson-Kimberly, 1904), 659. The fee apparently varied according to the situation. In an 1885 contract between the Francklyn Land and Cattle Company and John T. Lytle, the ranch agreed to furnish the remuda; otherwise the $1.00 per head rate would have been raised to $1.50. See Groom to Brown, February 26, 1885, in "B. B. Groom" File (Francklyn Records).
7. Pryor, "The Cost of Moving a Herd to Northern Markets," in Hunter (comp. and ed.), *Trail Drivers of Texas*, 367.
8. Ibid.
9. Ibid., 367–368.
10. As cited in Daniel Evander McArthur, "The Cattle Industry of Texas,

1685–1918" (M.A. thesis, University of Texas, 1918), 182; David B. Gracy, II, "George Washington Littlefield: Portrait of a Cattleman," *Southwestern Historical Quarterly*, LXVIII (October, 1964), 239.

11. "John T. Lytle," in Hunter (comp. and ed.), *Trail Drivers of Texas*, 322; Lomax to Stephens, July 8, [188]5, in Letters sent (Spur Records); J[ohn] H[enry] Stephens, Kyle, Texas, to Sommerville, Matador Ranch, March 1, 1885, in Headquarters Division, Letters received (Matador Records).

12. John S. Kritzer, "Lost Twenty-One Thousand Dollars on One Drive," in Hunter (comp. and ed.), *Trail Drivers of Texas*, 369.

13. [W. B. Slaughter?], "George Webb Slaughter," in ibid., 756.

14. Charles Goodnight, "More About the Chisholm Trail," in ibid., 951.

15. J. Evetts Haley, *Charles Goodnight, Cowman & Plainsman* (Boston: Houghton Mifflin Company, 1936), 260–276.

16. Rob[er]t Trogdon [?] to Samuel and M. J. Coggin, contract, September 10, 1873, in Legal documents, Coggin Brothers and Associates Records (Southwest Collection, Texas Tech University, Lubbock).

17. Lomax to G. H. Parrish, Swisher County, Tex[as], November 3, [188]5, in Letters sent (Spur Records).

18. Lomax to Mrs. S. A. Camel, Abilene, Tex[as], November 24, [188]5, in ibid.

19. Gard, *The Chisholm Trail*, 236–237.

20. W. F. Thompson, "My Trip up the Trail," in Hunter (comp. and ed.), *Trail Drivers of Texas*, 527–528; Jim Wilson, "Ate Stolen Meat, Anyway," in ibid., 464–465.

21. "A True Story of Trail Days," in ibid., 537–538. See also, John Wells, "Met Quanah Parker on the Trail," in ibid., 165.

22. Lomax to Stephens, Kansas City, Missouri, July 8, [188]5, in Letters sent (Spur Records); Sommerville to Mackay, Dec[ember] 14, [188]5, in Headquarters Division, Letters sent (Matador Records).

23. Sommerville to Mackay, January 23, [188]6, in Headquarters Division, Letters sent (Matador Records).

24. Sommerville to Mackay, Jan[uary] 1, 1884, in ibid.

25. T. Fred Harvey, "George Findlay, General Manager of the XIT Ranch, 1888–1889" (M.A. thesis, West Texas State College, 1950), 85–86.

26. Wayne Gard, "Retracing the Chisholm Trail," *Southwestern Historical Quarterly*, LX (July, 1956), 64.

27. W. Scott Schreiner, Kerrville, Texas, to JMS, August 23, 1965, in Jimmy M. Skaggs Papers (possession of the author).

28. John T. Lytle, San Antonio, Texas, to B. B. Groom, White Deer, Texas, April 14, 1885, in "B. B. Groom" File (Francklyn Records).

29. Trogdon [?] to Samuel and M. J. Coggin, September 10, 1873, in Legal documents (Coggin Brothers and Associates Records).

30. The Fort Griffin *Echo* and the [Dodge City] Ford County *Globe*, as did most trail-town newspapers, published weekly, monthly, and even yearly totals of trail herds driven to Kansas and elsewhere. A random check of these lists points up the frequency with which the names of trailing contractors appear. For example, see Fort Griffin *Echo*, May 21, 1879.

31. For a specific example, see L. B. Anderson, "Habits and Customs of Early Texans," in Hunter (comp. and ed.), *Trail Drivers of Texas*, 185.
32. Hunter (comp. and ed.), *Trail Drivers of Texas*, passim.

2
Lytle, McDaniel, Schreiner, and Light:
Entrepreneurs

1. Alice Lytle Gidley, Lytle, Texas, to JMS, August 12, 1965; San Antonio *Daily Light*, January 11, 1907; Helen Lytle to JMS (interview), April 2, 1966; "Captain John T. Lytle," in Hunter (comp. and ed.), *Trail Drivers of Texas*, 322; Leonard Lytle, "Outline of the Lytle Families of America," MS, 1932 (in Cincinnatti, Ohio, Public Library; copy in possession of the author), 94; Gus Ford (ed.), *Texas Cattle Brands* (Dallas: Clyde C. Cockrell Company, 1936), 212–213.

2. Dallas *Morning News*, January 11, 1907; [Freeman (ed.)], *Prose and Poetry of the Live Stock Industry of the United States*, 659.

3. Lewis Atherton, *The Cattle Kings* (Bloomington: Indiana University Press, 1961), 122.

4. Alice Lytle Gidley to JMS, June 1, 1965; Lytle to JMS (Interview), April 2, 1966; "Opening Session of the First National Cattle Growers' Association," in *Parson's Memorial and Historical Library Magazine*, I (1885), 301, 309. At an 1884 cattleman's convention in St. Louis, he was addressed as "Colonel Lytle."

5. Compiled Military Service Record for John T. Lytle, in War Department Collection of Confederate Records, Record Group 109 (National Archives, Washington); Compiled Military Service Record for Samuel Lytle, in ibid.

6. Jimmy M. Skaggs, "The Great Western Cattle Trail to Dodge City, Kansas" (M.A. thesis, Texas Technological College, 1965), 12–13; Alice Lytle Gidley to JMS, June 1, 1965; Lytle to JMS (interview), April 2, 1966; Ford (ed.), *Texas Cattle Brands*, 212–213; Lytle, "The Lytle Families," 94.

7. Alice Lytle Gidley to JMS, June 1, 1965; Lytle to JMS (interview), April 2, 1966; Ford (ed.), *Texas Cattle Brands*, 212–213. Helen Lytle wrote the brief sketch of her father for *Texas Cattle Brands*; the photograph she donated to be used in the Hall of the Cattle Kings, Texas Centennial Exposition, 1936 (a display for which the Ford book was designed as a guide), is permanently housed along with the other photographs of the Cattle Kings in the Museum, Texas Tech University.

8. Although the authoritative *Handbook of Texas* states that Lytle, Texas, was named in honor of William Lytle, Mayor T. E. Williams reports that his community was named for John T. Lytle because the cattleman donated land for public use. William Lytle's great granddaughter, Alice Lytle Gidley, and *The Trail Drivers of Texas* support Mayor Williams's contention. See, Walter Prescott Webb and H. Bailey Carroll (eds.), *The Handbook of Texas* (2 vols.; Austin: Texas State Historical Association,

1952), II, 98; "Captain John T. Lytle," in Hunter (comp. and ed.), *Trail Drivers of Texas*, 322; T. E. Williams, Lytle, Texas, to JMS, April 26, 1965; Alice Lytle Gidley to JMS, June 1, 1965.

9. "Captain John T. Lytle," in Hunter (comp. and ed.), *Trail Drivers of Texas*, 322; J. Evetts Haley, *Charles Schreiner, General Merchandise: The Story of a Country Store* (Austin: Texas State Historical Association, 1944), 45; Mrs. William J. Gidley, Baytown, Texas, to JMS, October 13, 1965.

10. Haley, *Charles Schreiner*, 1–5; Gene Hollon, "Captain Charles Schreiner: The Father of the Hill Country," *Southwestern Historical Quarterly*, XLVIII (October, 1944), 145–150.

11. Both Haley and Hollon cite profit figures far too low to allow Schreiner enough capital with which to purchase Faltin's interest; Schreiner's only other source of income at the time was from the trailing company. Haley, *Charles Schreiner*, 5–45; Hollon, "Captain Charles Schreiner: Father of the Hill Country," *Southwestern Historical Quarterly*, XLVIII, 150–158.

12. [James Cox (ed.)], *Historical and Biographical Record of the Cattle Industry* (St. Louis: Woodward & Tierman Printing Company, 1895), 657–658.

13. Ibid.

14. [Freeman (ed.)], *Prose and Poetry of the Live Stock Industry*, 659; Lester Field Sheffy, *The Francklyn Land and Cattle Company: A Panhandle Enterprise, 1882–1957* (Austin: Texas State Historical Association, 1964), 155–178. Helen Lytle states that her father always took his entire family with him when he journeyed to northern railheads. Lytle to JMS (interview), April 2, 1966.

15. Frank Collinson (comp. and ed. by Mary Whatley Clarke), *Life in the Saddle* (Norman: University of Oklahoma Press, 1963), 32–40; J. Wright Mooar, "Frontier Experiences of J. Wright Mooar," West Texas Historical Association *Year Book*, IV (June, 1928), 91; [Freeman (ed.)], *Prose and Poetry of the Live Stock Industry*, 659; Special Orders No. 102, May 3, 1872, in Records of the War Department, 4545½ Adjutant General's Office (AGO) for the year 1872 (filed with 4148 AGO 1872), Letters received, Record Group (RG) 94 (National Archives, Washington).

16. Ernest Wallace, *Ranald S. Mackenzie on the Texas Frontier* (Lubbock: West Texas Museum Association, 1964), 128ff; Jerry L. Rogers, " 'The Indian Territory Expedition' of Colonel Nelson Appleton Miles, 1874–1875" (M.A. thesis, Texas Technological College, 1965), 38ff.

17. "Captain John T. Lytle," in Hunter (comp. and ed.), *Trail Drivers of Texas*, 322; Ford (ed.), *Texas Cattle Brands*, 56.

18. Sheffy, *The Francklyn Land and Cattle Company*, 155–178; Philip Durham and Everett L. Jones, *The Negro Cowboys* (New York: Dodd, Mead & Company, 1965), 71–75.

19. Lytle to JMS (interview), April 2, 1966.

20. [Freeman (ed.)], *Prose and Poetry of the Live Stock Industry*, 660. Apparently Lytle's figures did not include the Francklyn Company's

25,000-head herd in 1885. See also, M. L. Cox, "Fort Griffin—Cowtown!" *The Cattleman*, L (March, 1965), 61, and Vernon Lynch, "1879 in the *Echo*: A Year at Fort Griffin on the Texas Frontier," West Texas Historical Association *Year Book*, XLI (October, 1965), 59.

21. "Captain Charles Schreiner," in Hunter (comp. and ed.), *Trail Drivers of Texas*, 362; Bob Bennett, *Kerr County, Texas: 1856–1956* (San Antonio: The Naylor Company, 1956); 42; Fort Griffin *Echo*, May 21, 1879.

22. Collinson, *Life in the Saddle*, 32–40; Joe Chapman, "An Old Frontiersman Tells His Experiences," in Hunter (comp. and ed.), *Trail Drivers of Texas*, 410–411; Oscar Thompson, "Were Happier in the Good Old Days," in ibid., 595; Sam Neill, "A Long Time Between Drinks," in ibid., 256–257; J. L. Hill, *The End of the Cattle Trail* (Long Beach: Geo. W. Moyle Publishing Co., [1923]), passim; Joe Montague to JMS, June 9, 1966. According to Mr. Montague, nephew of John T. Lytle, the boy's name was John Lytle Black.

23. Harry Sinclair Drago, *Great American Cattle Trails* (New York: Dodd, Mead & Company, 1965), 196.

24. Corwin Doan, "Reminiscences of the Trail," in Hunter (comp. and ed.), *Trail Drivers of Texas*, 777.

25. Drago, *Great American Cattle Trails*, 196.

26. Gus Black, "Had Plenty of Fun," in Hunter (comp. and ed.), *Trail Drivers of Texas*, 544.

27. Andy Adams, *Reed Anthony, Cowman: An Autobiography* (Boston: Houghton Mifflin and Company, 1907), 310–312.

28. Ibid., facing title page.

29. Collinson, *Life in the Saddle*, 48; Wilber S. Nye, *Carbine and Lance: The Story of Old Fort Sill* (Norman: University of Oklahoma Press, 1937), 296.

30. Although this story has been told and retold several times, there is no clearly original source for it. See Durham and Jones, *The Negro Cowboys*, 71–75; Harry E. Chrisman, *Lost Trails of the Cimarron* (Denver: Sage Books, 1964), 175–180; and Robert M. Wright, *Dodge City, The Cowboy Capital, and the Great Southwest* ([Wichita: Wichita *Eagle* Publishing Company, 1913]), 270–277.

31. Dale, *The Range Cattle Industry*, 8ff, 107ff.

32. Stephens, who then owned a trailing company in San Antonio, was apparently hired by Groom because of the immense size of the herd he planned to market; Groom evidently believed that two firms were necessary to handle 25,000 cattle adequately. Not much is known of Stephens's life or career. Born in North Carolina in 1829, he migrated to Texas about 1850, served with Terry's Texas Rangers during the Civil War, and began his cattle operations shortly thereafter. Stephens moved his commission business to Kansas City in 1883, where he resided at the time of his death on July 27, 1908. See Kansas City *Star*, July 27, 1908.

33. Groom to Brown, Feb[ruary] 26, 1885, in "B. B. Groom" File (Francklyn Records).

34. Ibid.

35. Sheffy, *The Francklyn Land and Cattle Company,* 155–178. Although it is not entirely clear, it is presumed that in this contractual agreement Lytle represented his entire firm.
36. [Freeman (ed.)], *Prose and Poetry of the Live Stock Industry,* 660; Haley, *Charles Schreiner,* 45–46; Bennett, *Kerr County, Texas,* 41.
37. [Cox (ed.)], *Historical and Biographical Record of the Cattle Industry,* 658.
38. Haley, *Charles Schreiner,* 46–70; Hollon, "Captain Charles Schreiner: Father of the Hill Country," *Southwestern Historical Quarterly,* XLVIII, 158–168.
39. The precise amount of the debt, said to have been immense, probably will never be known; even the Schreiner Company Records do not cast light on the subject. F. Scott Schreiner, Kerrville, Texas, to JMS, August 23, 1965; Lytle, "The Lytle Families," 94; Brian Montague (nephew of John T. Lytle), Del Rio, Texas, to JMS, July 25, August 2, 1966.
40. Estelle D. Tinkler, "Nobility's Ranche: A History of the Rocking Chair Ranche," *Panhandle-Plains Historical Review,* XV (1942), 13–17; Joe Montague to JMS, May 31, June 9, 1966; Brian Montague to JMS, July 25, August 2, 1966; George W. Saunders, "Reflections of the Trail," in Hunter (comp. and ed.), *Trail Drivers of Texas,* 449; Jasper Lauderdale, "Reminiscences of the Trail," in ibid., 409; [Freeman (ed.)], *Prose and Poetry of the Live Stock Industry,* 661.
41. *Texas State Gazetteer and Business Directory, 1892* (4 vols.; Detroit: R. L. Polk & Co., 1892), IV, 902, 1524; Saunders, "Reflections of the Trail," in Hunter (comp. and ed.), *Trail Drivers of Texas,* 449; Lauderdale, "Reminiscences of the Trail," in ibid., 409; Lottie Holman Card Papers (Southwest Collection, Texas Tech University); Alan A. Erwin, *The Southwest of John H. Slaughter, 1841–1922: Pioneer Cattleman and Trail-Driver of Texas, the Pecos, and Arizona, and Sheriff of Tombstone* (Glendale: The Arthur H. Clark Company, 1965), 73; Lytle, "The Lytle Families," 94; Gene M. Gressley, *Bankers and Cattlemen* (New York: Alfred A. Knopf, 1966), 262; "Thomas Jefferson Moore," in Hunter (comp. and ed.), *Trail Drivers of Texas,* 713. See also Skaggs, "John Thomas Lytle: Cattle Baron," *Southwestern Historical Quarterly,* LXXI, 57–60.

3
Consummate Conservative Contractor:
Eugene Bartlett Millett

1. Floyd Benjamin Streeter, "Longhorns, Shorthorns: The Life and Times of Captain Eugene Bartlett Millett, a Cattleman of the Old West," MS, n.d. (Special Collections, Ablah Library, Wichita State University), 1–10; Ellsworth [Kansas] *Messenger,* February 3, 1916. The series of articles in the Ellsworth *Messenger* cited herein were the result of several interviews of E. B. Millett by the newspaper's editor and obviously reflect Millett's personal evaluation of his life. Professor Streeter's manuscript, intended for publication, drew heavily upon interviews with

members of Millett's family; unfortunately, most of the sources cited by Streeter are no longer available.

2. Streeter, "The Life and Times of Captain Eugene Bartlett Millett," 11–12; Ellsworth [Kansas] *Messenger*, February 3, 1916.

3. Streeter, "The Life and Times of Captain Eugene Bartlett Millett," 14–28; Ellsworth [Kansas] *Messenger*, February 3, 1916.

4. Streeter, "The Life and Times of Captain Eugene Bartlett Millett," 13.

5. Ibid.; Ellsworth [Kansas] *Messenger*, February 3, 1916.

6. Ellsworth [Kansas] *Messenger*, February 3, 1916; "John and Thomas Dewees," in Hunter (comp. and ed.), *Trail Drivers of Texas*, 941.

7. Ellsworth [Kansas] *Messenger*, February 3, 1916; Streeter, "The Life and Times of Captain Eugene Bartlett Millett," 49.

8. Streeter, "The Life and Times of Captain Eugene Bartlett Millett," 49–52; Ellsworth [Kansas] *Messenger*, February 10, 1916; *Laws of the State of Missouri Passed at the Regular Session of the 21st General Assembly* (Jefferson City: W. G. Cheeney, Public Printer, 1861), 25–28; Joseph G. McCoy (Ralph P. Bieber, ed.), *Historic Sketches of the Cattle Trade of the West and Southwest* (Glendale: The Arthur H. Clark Company, 1940), 141–142.

9. Streeter, "The Life and Times of Captain Eugene Bartlett Millett," 62; Ellsworth [Kansas] *Messenger*, February 10, 1916; McCoy (Bieber, ed.), *Historic Sketches of the Cattle Trade*, 111–125.

10. Streeter, apparently basing his account at this point on the Ellsworth *Messenger*, states that Millett drove 500 cattle in 1868; McCoy recalled the total as 800; and Ralph Bieber, who edited McCoy's reprinted memoirs, found evidence that the herd numbered 950 head. Streeter, "The Life and Times of Captain Eugene Bartlett Millett," 62–63; Ellsworth [Kansas] *Messenger*, February 10, 1916; McCoy (Bieber, ed.), *Historic Sketches of the Cattle Trade*, 142. Millett in 1868 reportedly contemplated two additional drives, one 1,000-head herd going to California and another to the Dakotas. His failure to secure competent trail bosses apparently thwarted the venture. See F. G. Crawford, "Drove Horses to Mississippi," in Hunter (comp. and ed.), *Trail Drivers of Texas*, 634.

11. "Alonzo Millett," in Hunter (comp. and ed.), *Trail Drivers of Texas*, 815–816; Anderson, "Habits and Customs of Early Texans," in ibid., 184–185.

12. Streeter, "The Life and Times of Captain Eugene Bartlett Millett," 67–68; Ellsworth [Kansas] *Messenger*, February 10, 1916.

13. Streeter, "The Life and Times of Captain Eugene Bartlett Millett," 69; Ellsworth [Kansas] *Messenger*, February 10, 1916; McCoy (Bieber, ed.), *Historic Sketches of the Cattle Trade*, 143–144.

14. Streeter, "The Life and Times of Captain Eugene Bartlett Millett," 72; Ellsworth [Kansas] *Messenger*, February 17, 1916.

15. Streeter, "The Life and Times of Captain Eugene Bartlett Millett," 72–73; Ellsworth [Kansas] *Messenger*, February 17, 1916.

16. Streeter, "The Life and Times of Captain Eugene Bartlett Millett," 73–

75; Ellsworth [Kansas] *Messenger*, February 17, 1916; "Seth Mabry," in Hunter (comp. and ed.), *Trail Drivers of Texas*, 718.

17. Streeter, "The Life and Times of Captain Eugene Bartlett Millett," 75; Ellsworth [Kansas] *Messenger*, February 17, 1916; Cutbert Powell, *Twenty Years of Kansas City's Live Stock Trade and Traders* (Kansas City: Pearl Printing Company, 1893), 38–39.

18. L. B. Anderson, "A Few Thrilling Incidents in My Experience on the Trail," in Hunter (comp. and ed.), *Trail Drivers of Texas*, 205–206.

19. Streeter, "The Life and Times of Captain Eugene Bartlett Millett," 75–76; Ellsworth [Kansas] *Messenger*, February 24, 1916; Powell, *Twenty Years of Kansas City's Live Stock Trade and Traders*, 39.

20. Ellsworth [Kansas] *Messenger*, February 24, 1916.

21. Ibid.; Streeter, "The Life and Times of Captain Eugene Bartlett Millett," 87–88.

22. Streeter, "The Life and Times of Captain Eugene Bartlett Millett," 89–90; Ellsworth [Kansas] *Messenger*, February 24, 1916; J. F. Ellison, Jr., "Traveling the Trail with Good Men Was a Pleasure," in Hunter (comp. and ed.), *Trail Drivers of Texas*, 539; "R. G. (Dick) Head," in ibid., 734–736. Ellison, who trail bossed a herd for his father that followed one of the Millett-Mabry herds, recalled the year incorrectly as 1876. Too, Streeter asserts that the Millett-Mabry drive of 52,000 head in 1875 was the largest in history. Although one of the largest, it pales beside the 91,000-head drive of Lytle, McDaniel, Schreiner, and Light in 1884. Several other concerns equaled the Millett-Mabry feat.

23. Streeter, "The Life and Times of Captain Eugene Bartlett Millett," 90–110; Ellsworth [Kansas] *Messenger*, March 2, 9, 16, 28, 1916.

24. Streeter, "The Life and Times of Captain Eugene Bartlett Millett," 112–118.

25. Ibid., 164–169.

4
The Family Enterprises

1. [Henry Ford], "Coggin & Bro.," in [Cox (ed.)], *Historical and Biographical Record of the Cattle Industry*, 364; Frank Collinson, El Paso, Texas, to Bruce, Gerdes, Tulia, Texas, October 11, 1938, in Frank Collinson Papers (Southwest Collection, Texas Tech University, Lubbock).

2. [Ford], "Coggin & Bro.," in [Cox (ed.)], *Historical and Biographical Record of the Cattle Industry*. 364.

3. Ibid.; Trogdon [?] to Samuel and M. J. Coggin, September 10, 1873, in Legal Documents (Coggin Brothers and Associates Records); Kritzer, "Lost Twenty-One Thousand Dollars on One Drive," in Hunter (comp. and ed.), *Trail Drivers of Texas*, 369.

4. [Ford], "Coggin & Bro.," in [Cox (ed.)], *Historical and Biographical Record of the Cattle Industry*, 364; McArthur, "The Cattle Industry of Texas, 1685–1918," 118–120.

5. [Ford], "Coggin & Bro.," in [Cox (ed.)], *Historical and Biographical*

Record of the Cattle Industry, 364–365; Powell, Twenty Years of Kansas City's Live Stock Trade and Traders, 38.

6. [Ford], "Coggin & Bro.," in [Cox (ed.)], Historical and Biographical Record of the Cattle Industry, 365; Collinson, Life in the Saddle, 115–116, 139–140.

7. [Ford], "Coggin & Bro.," in [Cox (ed.)], Historical and Biographical Record of the Cattle Industry, 365; Jimmy M. Skaggs, "A Study in Business Failure: Frank Collinson in the Big Bend," Panhandle-Plains Historical Review, XLIII (1970), 9–20.

8. Webb and Carroll (eds.), The Handbook of Texas, I, 176, credit John Blocker with running the federal blockade during the Civil War by driving ox-teams to and from Mexico; however, Claude Elliott, "Union Sentiment in Texas, 1861–1865," Southwestern Historical Quarterly, L (April, 1947), 467, lists Abner P. Blocker, Sr., as a leader of the Travis County, Texas, unionist group, which strenuously opposed Texas's secession.

9. "One of the Best Known Trail Drivers," in Hunter (comp. and ed.), Trail Drivers of Texas, 319; E. C. Abbott, "John R. Blocker, King of the Texas Trail," Frontier Times, XIV (August, 1937), 497. Abbott, better known to drovers as Teddy Blue, was active in the cattle industry and became a close friend of J. R. Blocker's.

10. John R. Blocker, "The Trail Drivers of Texas," in Hunter (comp. and ed.), Trail Drivers of Texas, 2.

11. Quoted in J. Frank Dobie, "Ab Blocker: Trail Boss," Arizona and the West, VI (Summer, 1964), 98.

12. Ibid.

13. Abbott, "John R. Blocker, King of the Texas Trail," Frontier Times, XIV, 497.

14. "William Henry Jennings," in History of the Cattlemen of Texas (Dallas: The Johnson Printing and Advertising Company, 1914), 283; Ford (ed.), Texas Cattle Brands, 221–222; "William Henry Jennings," in Hunter (comp. and ed.), Trail Drivers of Texas, 915–916.

15. "William Henry Jennings," in Hunter (comp. and ed.), Trail Drivers of Texas, 916; J. R. Jennings, "Cowboys Dressed up at the End of the Trail," in ibid., 535. At one time Jennings also was associated with J. F. Ellison in buying and trailing cattle. See, W. B. Hardman, "Tells about Bob Robertson," in ibid., 796; F. M. Polk, "My Experiences on the Cow Trail," in ibid., 142–143.

16. Ab[ner P.] Blocker, "The Man Who Had Hell in His Neck," in ibid., 504–506; Abbott, "John R. Blocker, King of the Texas Trail," Frontier Times, XIV, 497; Polk, "My Experiences on the Cow Trail," in Hunter (comp. and ed.), Trail Drivers of Texas, 142; J. Marvin Hunter, "Ab Blocker and the XIT," Frontier Times, XXI (October, 1943), 42–43.

17. Blocker, "The Man Who Had Hell in His Neck," in Hunter (comp. and ed.), Trail Drivers of Texas, 506, gives the date as 1884, but all other sources clearly indicate the drive occurred in 1885. See Webb and Carroll (eds.), The Handbook of Texas, II, 490; "One of the Best Known Trail Drivers," in Hunter (comp. and ed.), Trail Drivers of

Texas, 321; and J. Evetts Haley, *The XIT Ranch of Texas and the Early Days of the Llano Estacado* (Chicago: The Lakeside Press, 1929), 81.

18. Hunter, "Ab Blocker and the XIT," *Frontier Times*, XXI, 43.

19. Ibid.; [Abner P. Blocker], "Ab Blocker Tells about Trail Driving Days," in ibid., V (October, 1927), 20–21. Although folklore has obscured the origin (and meaning) of the XIT brand, there is no disagreement among authorities regarding Blocker's role in creating the mark.

20. [Blocker], "Ab Blocker Tells about Trail Driving Days," *Frontier Times*, V, 21 See also, Blocker, "The Man Who Had Hell in His Neck," in Hunter (comp. and ed.), *Trail Drivers of Texas*, 507–508; "One of the Best Known Trail Drivers," in ibid., 321; and, *History of the Cattlemen of Texas*, 65.

21. Blocker, "The Man Who Had Hell in His Neck," in Hunter (comp. and ed.), *Trail Drivers of Texas*, 510.

22. Hunter, "Ab Blocker and the XIT," *Frontier Times*, XXI, 43.

23. Quoted in Hunter (comp. and ed.), *Trail Drivers of Texas*, 553.

24. G. M. Carson, "When Ab Blocker Climbed a Fence," in ibid., 251.

25. Abbott, "John R. Blocker, King of the Texas Trail," *Frontier Times*, XIV, 497–498; see also, Dobie, "Ab Blocker: Trail Boss," *Arizona and the West*, VI, 100.

26. Blocker, "The Man Who Had Hell in His Neck," in Hunter (comp. and ed.), *Trail Drivers of Texas*, 512.

27. Ibid., 504–506; Joe P. Smith, "Made Several Trips," in ibid., 862; G. M. Mills, "Experiences 'Tenderfeet' Could Not Survive," in ibid., 238.

28. A number of sources were consulted to obtain this compiled figure: Blocker, "The Man Who Had Hell in His Neck," in ibid., 505–513; "William Henry Jennings," in ibid., 915–916; and Abbott, "John R. Blocker, King of the Texas Trail," *Frontier Times*, XIV, 497–498.

29. Abbott, "John R. Blocker, King of the Texas Trail," *Frontier Times*, XIV, 497–498, for example, states that the concern trailed some 45,000 cattle northward in 1881, whereas other sources, especially Ab Blocker, mention only 6,000 to 9,000 head on the trail that year; similarly, Faun Vernon Strout, "The History and Development of Education in Wilbarger County from 1858 to 1937" (M.A. thesis, Southern Methodist University, 1937), 10, cites 90,000 cattle moved by the Blockers in 1885 as opposed to the 25,000 head mentioned by Ab Blocker. See Blocker, "The Man Who Had Hell in His Neck," in Hunter (comp. and ed.), *Trail Drivers of Texas*, 505–513.

30. Hunter, "Ab Blocker and the XIT," *Frontier Times*, XXI, 43. Hunter and Blocker were close, personal friends, and doubtless Hunter's estimation was based on personal conversations with Blocker.

31. B. H. Campbell, XIT Ranch, to Webb & Webb, Albany, Texas, Feb[ruary] 22, 1886, in "B. B. Campbell Correspondence File," XIT Ranch Records (Archives, Panhandle-Plains Historical Museum, Canyon, Texas).

32. Blocker, "The Man Who Had Hell in His Neck," in Hunter (comp. and ed.), *Trail Drivers of Texas*, 512; Ford (ed.), *Texas Cattle Brands*, 223; Dobie, "Ab Blocker: Trail Boss, *Arizona and the West*, VI, 98.

33. "The Remarkable Career of Colonel Ike T. Pryor," in Hunter (comp. and ed.), *Trail Drivers of Texas*, 174; J. Marvin Hunter, "Ike T. Pryor was a Great Cattleman," *Frontier Times*, XXVI (October, 1948), 129; C. L. Douglas, *Cattle Kings of Texas* (Dallas: Cecil Baugh, 1939), 246. It appears certain that if Pryor did not pen the piece for the *Trail Drivers of Texas* himself, he at least supplied J. Marvin Hunter with the information; as in the case of Hunter and Ab Blocker, Hunter and Pryor were also close, personal friends. The Douglas account of Pryor's life was based entirely on a 1936 interview with the cattleman.

34. "The Remarkable Career of Colonel Ike T. Pryor," in Hunter (comp. and ed.), *Trail Drivers of Texas*, 174–178.

35. "David C. Pryor," in ibid., 706; Dallas *Morning News*, September 25, 1937; Douglas, *Cattle Kings of Texas*, 250–251; Ike T. Pryor, Untitled address before the Thirty-eighth Annual Meeting of the Cattle Raisers Association, Fort Worth, Texas, March 10, 1914, in Ike T. Pryor Papers (Archives, University of Texas at Austin); "The Remarkable Career of Colonel Ike T. Pryor," in Hunter (comp. and ed.), *Trail Drivers of Texas*, 178.

36. Pryor, Untitled address, March 10, 1914 (Pryor Papers).

37. Quoted in Douglas, *Cattle Kings of Texas*, 251. Pryor told and retold this episode several times, and although the story remained unchanged, his exact statement to Cain varies with the telling. For example, see J. Frank Dobie, "Hunting Cousin Sally," *Southwest Review*, XLVIII (Summer, 1963), 184.

38. Douglas, *Cattle Kings of Texas*, 251; Dallas *Morning News*, September 25, 1937.

39. Quoted in Douglas, *Cattle Kings of Texas*, 251.

40. Ibid; [Freeman (ed.)], *Prose and Poetry of the Live Stock Industry*, 104; "The Remarkable Career of Colonel Ike T. Pryor," in Hunter (comp. and ed.), *Trail Drivers of Texas*, 178.

41. [Freeman (ed.)], *Prose and Poetry of the Live Stock Industry*, 104; "The Remarkable Career of Colonel Ike T. Pryor," in Hunter (comp. and ed.), *Trail Drivers of Texas*, 178; Douglas, *Cattle Kings of Texas*, 252.

42. [Freeman (ed.)], *Prose and Poetry of the Live Stock Industry*, 104; Douglas, *Cattle Kings of Texas*, 252; "The Remarkable Career of Colonel Ike T. Pryor," in Hunter (comp. and ed.), *Trail Drivers of Texas*, 178.

43. [Jack Jones], as told to Ruth Hunnicutt, "Plain Talk from Jack Jones," *The Cattleman*, XXXII (October, 1945), 131.

44. "The Remarkable Career of Colonel Ike T. Pryor," in Hunter (comp. and ed.), *Trail Drivers of Texas*, 178; [Freeman (ed.)], *Prose and Poetry of the Live Stock Industry*, 660.

45. "The Remarkable Career of Colonel Ike T. Pryor," in Hunter (comp. and ed.), *Trail Drivers of Texas*, 178–179; Pryor, "The Cost of Moving a Herd to Northern Markets," in ibid., 367; Douglas, *Cattle Kings of Texas*, 252.

46. Pryor, "The Cost of Moving a Herd to Northern Markets," in Hunter (comp. and ed.), *Trail Drivers of Texas*, 367.

47. Ibid.
48. [Jones] as told to Hunnicutt, "Plain Talk from Jack Jones," *The Cattle-man*, XXXII, 131.
49. Ibid.
50. Ibid.
51. Pryor, "The Cost of Moving a Herd to Northern Markets," in Hunter (comp. and ed.), *Trail Drivers of Texas*, 367.
52. [Jones] as told to Hunnicutt, "Plain Talk from Jack Jones," *The Cattle-man*, XXXII, 132; Pryor, "The Cost of Moving a Herd to Northern Markets," in Hunter (comp. and ed.), *Trail Drivers of Texas*, 367–368.
53. [Freeman (ed.)], *Prose and Poetry of the Live Stock Industry*, 105.
54. Douglas, *Cattle Kings of Texas*, 252–253.
55. Ibid., 253–254; [Freeman (ed.)], *Prose and Poetry of the Live Stock Industry*, 104; Dallas *Morning News*, September 25, 1937; Ellis A. Davis and Edwin H. Grobe (comp. and eds.), *The New Encyclopedia of Texas* (5 vols.; Dallas: Texas Development Bureau, [1929]), I, 474–475.

5
Horizontal, Vertical, or Conglomerate

1. J. F. Ellison, Jr., "Sketch of Colonel J. F. Ellison," in Hunter (comp. and ed.), *Trail Drivers of Texas*, 476–477.
2. Ibid. See also Ellison, "Traveling the Trail with Good Men Was a Pleasure," in ibid., 358.
3. Ellison, "Sketch of Colonel J. F. Ellison," in ibid., 477.
4. Ibid., 476–477; Ellison, "Traveling the Trail with Good Men Was a Pleasure," in ibid., 358.
5. If the new concern ever selected a title for itself, evidence of such has not been found. Whatever its official name, it was simply known throughout the range cattle kingdom as "Ellison and Dewees." See Hunter (comp. and ed.), *Trail Drivers of Texas*, passim.
6. According to J. F. Ellison, Jr., "Sketch of Colonel J. F. Ellison," in ibid., 478, the Ellison and Dewees partnership was abrogated in 1877. Over-whelming evidence to the contrary, however, places the date much later. See Hunter (comp. and ed.), *Trail Drivers of Texas*, passim.
7. This compiled figure is derived from various independent yearly totals as reported in ibid., passim, and from Gard, "Retracing the Chisholm Trail," *Southwestern Historical Quarterly*, LX, 64. Specifically see: Ellison, "Sketch of Colonel J. F. Ellison," in Hunter (comp. and ed.), *Trail Drivers of Texas*, 476–478; Ellison, "Traveling the Trail with Good Men Was a Pleasure," in ibid., 538–540; J. F. Ellison, Jr., "Made Several Trips up the Trail," in ibid., 92–93; George W. Saunders, "John and Thomas Dewees," in ibid., 940–942; L. B. Anderson, "A Few Thrilling Incidents in My Experiences on the Trail," in ibid., 203–207; "Alonzo Millett," in ibid., 815–816; W. F. Fielder, "When Elements Wept and Shed Tears," in ibid., 688–690; Leo Tucker, "Kidnapped the Inspec-tors," in ibid., 704–705; "William G. Butler," in ibid., 715–718; C. C. French, "When the Temperature Was 72 Below Zero," in ibid., 742–743;

W. T. Jackman, "Where They Put a Trail Boss in Jail," ibid., 856–859; Richard Withers, "The Experiences of an Old Trail Driver," in ibid., 305–315; "R. G. (Dick) Head," in ibid., 734–736; E. M. Story, "Got Their Names in the Pot for Supper and Breakfast," in ibid., 491–494; Jennings, "Cowboys Dressed up at the End of the Trail," in ibid., 534–536; Jeff Connolly, "Hit the Trail in High Places," in ibid., 188; J. M. Handins, "Reminiscences of Old Trail Driving," in ibid., 113–114; Anderson, "Habits and Customs of Early Texas," in ibid., 185; Mills, "Experiences 'Tenderfeet' Could Not Survive," in ibid., 230–236; Thomas Welder, "Preferred to Take Older Cattle up the Trail," in ibid., 294–295; and "Texas Collection," *Southwestern Historical Quarterly*, XLIV (July, 1940), 130.

8. Saunders, "John and Thomas Dewees," in Hunter (comp. and ed.), *Trail Drivers of Texas*, 941; Ellison, "Traveling the Trail with Good Men Was a Pleasure," in ibid., 539. See above, Chapter 3.

9. Withers, "The Experiences of an Old Time Trail Driver," in ibid., 316; "R. G. (Dick) Head," in ibid., 735; Anderson, "A Few Thrilling Incidents in My Experiences on the Trail," in ibid., 203; Jackman, "Where They Put a Trail Boss in Jail," in ibid., 856.

10. "Sketch of J. M. Choate," in ibid., 736; "W. M. Choate," in ibid., 738; W. D. H. Saunders, "Drove a Herd to Mississippi and Alabama," in ibid., 267–268; J. M. Byler, "Got 'Wild and Woolly' on the Chisholm Trail," in ibid., 114. Byler states that B. A. Borroum was Choate's partner on this drive, an error repeated by Wayne Gard, "The Shawnee Trail," *Southwestern Historical Quarterly*, LVI (January, 1953), 370. Ben A. Borroum, however, appears to have been the son of James Borroum (Choate's associate). At any rate, B. A. Borroum himself acknowledges that he merely worked for Choate and Borroum and that his first trip as a drover did not occur until 1870. See, B. A. Borroum, "Recollections of Old Trail Days," in Hunter (comp. and ed.), *Trail Drivers of Texas*, 117–119.

11. Borroum, "Recollections of Old Trail Days," in ibid., 117–119; George W. Saunders, "Origin and Close of the Old-Time Northern Trail," in ibid., 22.

12. McCoy (Bieber, ed.), *Historic Sketches of the Cattle Trade*, 144–145; Sam Garner, "Paid Three Dollars for Five Gallons of Water," in Hunter (comp. and ed.), *Trail Drivers of Texas*, 520; Withers, "Experiences of an Old Trail Driver," in ibid., 305; "R. G. (Dick) Head," in ibid., 734.

13. Garner, "Paid Three Dollars for Five Gallons of Water," in ibid., 734; "Sketch of Colonel J. J. Myers," in ibid., 637; McCoy (Bieber, ed.), *Historic Sketches of the Cattle Trade*, 146–147.

14. The nickname Shanghai reportedly resulted from Pierce's gangling appearance as a youth; the long-necked youngster reminded some of a Shanghai rooster. See Gard, *The Chisholm Trail*, 25, and Chris Emmett, *Shanghai Pierce: A Fair Likeness* (Norman: University of Oklahoma Press, 1953), passim.

15. [George W. Saunders], "Shanghai Pierce," in Hunter (comp. and ed.), *Trail Drivers of Texas*, 923–924.

16. [Cox (ed.)], *Historical and Biographical Record of the Cattle Industry*, 613; "Colonel Dillard R. Fant," in Hunter (comp. and ed.), *Trail Drivers of Texas*, 515–517.
17. N. L. Word, "Made Several Trips up the Trail," in ibid., 383; James Marion Garner, "Some Trips up the Trail," in ibid., 585; L. T. Clark, "Worked for George W. Saunders in 1875," in ibid., 562; [Cox (ed.)], *Historical and Biographical Record of the Cattle Industry*, 613.
18. [Cox (ed.)], *Historical and Biographical Record of the Cattle Industry*, 613; James T. Johnson, "Hardship of a Cowboy's Life in the Early Days of Texas," in Hunter (comp. and ed.), *Trail Drivers of Texas*, 761; J. M. Custer, "Scouting and Routing in the Good Old Days," in ibid., 257; Samuel Dunn Houston, "A Trying Trip Alone through the Wilderness," in ibid., 78–88; C. E. Johnson, "Could Ride a Hundred Miles in a Day," in ibid., 817–819; "Colonel Dillard R. Fant," in ibid., 517; J. R. Humphries, "From the Nueces to the North Platte," in ibid., 805.
19. "Colonel Dillard R. Fant," in ibid., 517; [Cox (ed.)], *Historical and Biographical Record of the Cattle Industry*, 613.
20. [Cox (ed.)], *Historical and Biographical Record of the Cattle Industry*, 613–614; Ford (ed.), *Texas Cattle Brands*, 224–225.
21. "George W. West," in Hunter (comp. and ed.), *Trail Drivers of Texas*, 834–835; "Sketch of L. B. Allen," in ibid., 525; Humphries, "From the Nueces to the North Platte," in ibid., 802; Tucker, "Kidnapped the Inspectors," in ibid., 703; Hiram G. Craig, "Days Gone By," in ibid., 338.
22. [Sol West], "Courage and Hardihood on the Old Texas Cattle Trail," in ibid., 128–129.
23. Ibid., 131.
24. "George W. West," in ibid., 835–836; Humphries, "From the Nueces to the North Platte," in ibid., 802–806; "One of the Best Known Trail Drivers," in ibid., 321; Blocker, "The Man Who Had Hell in His Neck," in ibid., 506–507.
25. Saunders, "Reflections of the Trail," in ibid., 430.
26. Ibid.
27. Ibid., 434.
28. Ibid. Saunders's reminiscences from the *Trail Drivers of Texas* were reproduced as J. Marvin Hunter, "George Saunders's First Trip," *Frontier Times*, V (May, 1928), 321–324.
29. Saunders, "Reflections of the Trail," in Hunter (comp. and ed.), *Trail Drivers of Texas*, 437–439.
30. H. C. Williams, "Took Time to Visit his Sweetheart," in ibid., 403.
31. Ibid.; Saunders, "Reflections of the Trail," in ibid., 439–440.
32. Saunders, "Reflections of the Trail," in ibid., 440.
33. Ibid., 439–440.
34. Ibid., 440–441.
35. Ibid., 441; Hawkins, "When George Saunders Made a Bluff Stick," in ibid, 391.
36. Saunders, "Reflections of the Trail," in ibid., 447.
37. Ibid.
38. Ibid., 448–449.

39. Ibid., 449.
40. Ibid.
41. His associates in this enterprise were a Dr. Graves, John T. Lytle, Jesse Presnall, John Price, W. H. Jennings, and Thomas Jefferson Moore. Ibid.
42. Ibid., 449–450.
43. See, Haley, *Charles Schreiner, General Merchandise*, passim; Hollon, "Captain Charles Schreiner: The Father of the Hill Country," *Southwestern Historical Quarterly*, XLVIII, 145–168.
44. "Thomas Jefferson Moore," in Hunter (comp. and ed.), *Trail Drivers of Texas*, 712–714.
45. J. Evetts Haley, *George W. Littlefield, Texan* (Norman: University of Oklahoma Press, 1943), 200–205; David B. Gracy, II, *Littlefield Lands: Colonization on the Texas Plains, 1912–1920* (Austin: University of Texas Press, 1968), 7; George Findlay, XIT Ranch, to A. G. Boyce, n.p., May 17, 1901, in "Boyce-Findlay Letter File" (XIT Records).
46. J. R. Blocker (b. 1851), J. S. Chisum (b. 1828), J. M. Choate (b. 1822), M. J. Coggin (b. 1824), S. R. Coggin (b. 1831), J. O. Dewees (b. 1828), J. F. Ellison (b. 1828), D. F. Fant (b. 1841), C. Goodnight (b. 1836), J. W. Light (b. 1844), G. W. Littlefield (b. 1842), O. Loving (b. 1812), J. T. Lytle (b. 1844), T. M. McDaniel (?), S. Mabry (?), J. J. Myers (?), E. B. Millett (b. 1838), A. H. Pierce (b. 1834), I. T. Pryor (b. 1852), G. W. Saunders (b. 1854), C. A. Schreiner (b. 1838), J. H. Stephens (b. 1829).

6

At the End of the Trail:
Marketing

1. Helen Lytle to JMS (interview), April 2, 1966.
2. McCoy (Bieber, ed.), *Historic Sketches of the Cattle Trade*, 112.
3. Ibid., 272. The railroad, McCoy charges in his autobiography, later repudiated its agreement and refused to pay him for the cattle shipped in 1869. For details of the dispute, see ibid., 267–286.
4. Ibid., 329–330; Powell, *Twenty Years of Kansas City's Live Stock Trade and Traders*, 15, 38.
5. Powell, *Twenty Years of Kansas City's Live Stock Trade and Traders*, 14–21.
6. Ibid., 38.
7. McCoy (Bieber, ed.), *Historic Sketches of the Cattle Trade*, 333–334.
8. Ibid.; Powell, *Twenty Years of Kansas City's Live Stock Trade and Traders*, 15–25.
9. McCoy (Bieber, ed.), *Historic Sketches of the Cattle Trade*, 334.
10. Ibid., 334–346.
11. Powell, *Twenty Years of Kansas City's Live Stock Trade and Traders*, 17, 175–177.
12. Ibid., 174; McCoy (Bieber, ed.), *Historic Sketches of the Cattle Trade*, 335.
13. McCoy (Bieber, ed.), *Historic Sketches of the Cattle Trade*, 336–337;

Powell, *Twenty Years of Kansas City's Live Stock Trade and Traders*, 175–176, 195–196.

14. Powell, *Twenty Years of Kansas City's Live Stock Trade and Traders*, 70–73.

15. McCoy (Bieber, ed.), *Historic Sketches of the Cattle Trade*, 102–103; "Biographical Sketches: Col. R. D. Hunter," in *Parson's Memorial and Historical Library Magazine*, I, 319; Mary Jane Gentry, "Thurber: The Life and Death of a Texas Town" (M.A. thesis, University of Texas, 1946), 11.

16. "Biographical Sketches: Col. R. D. Hunter," in *Parson's Memorial and Historical Library Magazine*, I, 103–104; McCoy (Bieber, ed.), *Historic Sketches of the Cattle Trade*, 103–104.

17. McCoy (Bieber, ed.), *Historic Sketches of the Cattle Trade*, 104–106.

18. Ibid., 106; "Biographical Sketches: Col. R. D. Hunter," in *Parson's Memorial and Historical Library Magazine*, I, 320.

19. McCoy (Bieber, ed.), *Historic Sketches of the Cattle Trade*, 106; "Biographical Sketches: Col. R. D. Hunter," in *Parson's Memorial and Historical Library Magazine*, I, 320.

20. "Biographical Sketches: Col. R. D. Hunter," in *Parson's Memorial and Historical Library Magazine*, I, 320; "Biographical Sketches: Capt. Albert G. Evans," in ibid., 325; "The Firm of Hunter, Evans & Co., in ibid., 325; Powell, *Twenty Years of Kansas City's Live Stock Trade and Traders*, 210.

21. "Biographical Sketches: Capt. Albert G. Evans," in *Parson's Memorial and Historical Library Magazine*, I, 324–325; Powell, *Twenty Years of Kansas City's Live Stock Trade and Traders*, 209–210.

22. "Biographical Sketches: Capt. Albert G. Evans," in *Parson's Memorial and Historical Library Magazine*, I, 325.

23. Gentry, "Thurber: The Life and Death of a Texas Town," 12.

24. Quoted in ibid., 13. See also Johnny Franks, Mengus, Texas, to Charles Townsend (interview), April 1, 1967 (Oral History File, Southwest Collection, Texas Tech University).

25. "The Firm of Hunter, Evans & Co.," in *Parson's Memorial and Historical Library Magazine*, I, 325; Powell, *Twenty Years of Kansas City's Live Stock Trade and Traders*, 179–180, 304.

26. "The Firm of Hunter, Evans & Co.," in *Parson's Memorial and Historical Library Magazine*, I, 325; Powell, *Twenty Years of Kansas City's Live Stock Trade and Traders*, 180–181; Marjorie Kinney, Head, Missouri Valley Room, Kansas City (Missouri) Public Library, to JMS, March 11, 1972.

27. "The Firm of Hunter, Evans & Co.," in *Parson's Memorial and Historical Library Magazine*, I, 325–326; Gentry, "Thurber: The Life and Death of a Texas Town," 11; Nimmo, *Report on Range and Ranch Cattle Traffic*, 21–22; Grover Cleveland to the Senate of the United States, December 21, 1885, and Legislation Enacted therewith, in U.S. Congress, *Executive Document No. 14*, 49th Cong., 1st Sess. (1885–1886), 1–6.

28. "The Firm of Hunter, Evans & Co.," in *Parson's Memorial and Historical*

Library Magazine, I, 325; Powell, *Twenty Years of Kansas City's Live Stock Trade and Traders*, 181, 305; Gentry, "Thurber: The Life and Death of a Texas Town," 11.

29. Gentry, "Thurber: The Life and Death of a Texas Town," 11–15; Robert William Spode, "W. W. Johnson and the Beginning of Coal Mining in the Strawn-Thurber Vicinity, 1880–1888," West Texas Historical Association *Year Book*, XLIV (October, 1968), 48–59.

30. McCoy (Bieber, ed.), *Historic Sketches of the Cattle Trade*, 360–361; Powell, *Twenty Years of Kansas City's Live Stock Trade and Traders*, 86–87. Slavens once associated in business with Eugene B. Millett. See above, Chapter 3.

31. Powell, *Twenty Years of Kansas City's Live Stock Trade and Traders*, 86–87.

32. Ibid., 89–91; McCoy, *Historic Sketches of the Cattle Trade*, 348–349.

33. Powell, *Twenty Years of Kansas City's Live Stock Trade and Traders*, 91–93.

34. Ibid., 88–95.

7
The Economic Impact of Trailing

1. Quoted in Edward Everett Dale, *Cow Country* (Norman: University of Oklahoma Press, 1942), 140.

2. U.S. Congress, House, *Report No. 1228*, 49th Cong., 1st Sess. (1885–1886).

3. Quoted in Dale, *The Range Cattle Industry*, 64.

4. *Guide Map of the Great Texas Cattle Trail from Red River Crossing to the Old Reliable Kansas Pacific Railway* (N.p.: Kansas Pacific Railway Co., 1875), 8ff; Nimmo, *Report on Range and Ranch Cattle Traffic*, 31. See Robert R. Dykstra, *The Cattle Towns* (New York: Alfred A. Knopf, 1968), 170, for additional details regarding surviving copies of these rare pieces of Americana.

5. U.S. Bureau of the Census, *Statistics of the Population of the United States at the Ninth Census* (Washington: Government Printing Office, 1884), 1186–1187; Bessie Louise Pierce, *A History of Chicago: The Rise of a Modern City* (3 vols.; New York: Alfred A. Knopf, 1937–1957), 108–144.

6. For the best treatment of the impact of the cattle trails on the railhead-markets, see Dykstra, *The Cattle Towns*, passim.

7. McCoy (Bieber, ed.), *Historic Sketches of the Cattle Trade*, 205–209.

8. Freight rates quoted in Ruth G. Newman, "The Industrialization of Fort Worth" (M.A. thesis, North Texas State College, 1950), 53–54. See also, Dykstra, *The Cattle Towns*, 81.

9. Fort Worth *Democrat*, April 24, 1875.

10. Nimmo, *Report on Range and Ranch Cattle Traffic*, 31; Gard, *The Chisholm Trail*, 227–228; Drago, *Great American Cattle Trails*, 193ff.

11. J. L. McCaleb, "My First Five Dollar Bill," in Hunter (comp. and ed.), *Trail Drivers of Texas*, 486–487; Dykstra, *The Cattle Towns*, 104; Nyle

H. Miller and Joseph W. Snell, *Great Gunfighters of the Kansas Cowtowns* (Lincoln: University of Nebraska Press, 1963), 78–79.

12. McCoy (Bieber, ed.), *Historic Sketches of the Cattle Trade*, 206; Jack Allen Shefrin, "The Chisholm Trail" (M.A. thesis, University of Kansas City, 1940), 65; Nimmo, *Report on Range and Ranch Cattle Traffic*, 31.

13. McCoy (Bieber, ed.), *Historic Sketches of the Cattle Trade*, 291–297.

14. R. M. Wright, "Early Days in Dodge City," *Frontier Times*, 26 (September, 1949), 317–322.

15. Glynn Mitchell, "History of Coleman County" (M.A. thesis, University of Texas, 1949), 67–74.

16. San Angelo *Standard Times*, August 29, 1954; James T. Padgitt, "Early Days in Coleman," West Texas Historical Association *Year Book*, XXVIII (October, 1952), 82; U.S. Bureau of the Census, *Statistics of the Population of the United States at the Tenth Census*, 63–64; U.S. Bureau of the Census, *Compendium of the Eleventh Census: 1890* (Washington: Government Printing Office, 1892), Pt. I, 389.

17. Collinson, *Life in the Saddle*, 35; Jack Potter (Laura R. Krehbiel, ed.), *Cattle Trails of the Old West* (Clayton, N.M.: Laura R. Krehbiel, 1939), 18; John Myres Myres, *Doc Holliday* (Boston: Little, Brown and Company, 1955), 65; Ben O. Grant, "Life in Old Fort Griffin," West Texas Historical Association *Year Book*, X (October, 1934), 34.

18. Ben O. Grant, "The Early History of Shackelford County" (M.A. thesis, Hardin-Simmons University, 1936), 84–85. Mr. Grant's study was based largely on his survey of county court records. See also, J. Marvin Hunter, *The Story of Lottie Deno: Her Life and Times* (Bandera, Texas: The 4 Hunters, 1959), passim.

19. Grant, "The Early History of Shackelford County," 84–85.

20. Collinson, *Life in the Saddle*, 67.

21. Collinson, El Paso, Texas, to Bruce Gerdes, Tulia, Texas, October 11, 1938 (Collinson Papers).

22. A. P. Black, *The End of the Long Horn Trail* (N.p.: n.p., n.d.), 8; U.S. Bureau of the Census, *Compendium of the Eleventh Census: 1890*, Pt. I, 387.

23. James D. Hamlin, "Recollections," MS, 1946, Set I, 118–121; Set II, 62–65, in James D. Hamlin Papers (Southwest Collection, Texas Tech University, Lubbock).

24. U.S. Bureau of the Census, *Statistics of the Population of the United States at the Tenth Census*, 63–64; Webb and Carroll (eds.), *The Handbook of Texas*, I, 24–25; Peter Hart, *Description of Shackelford County, State of Texas, U.S.A.: Its Creation, Organization, Wealth, and Productiveness, with a Synopsis of Its Soil, Climate, Products, Etc.* (Albany, Texas: Shackelford County, 1886), not paged.

25. For a fuller treatment of this frontier business enterprise, see Jimmy M. Skaggs, "Frontier Business Diversification: The Webb and Hill Company of Albany, Texas," West Texas Historical Association *Year Book*, XLIV (October, 1968), 26–37.

26. Louis Hamilton Hill, Biographical Data Sheet (Southwest Collection, Texas Tech University, Lubbock).

27. *The Breeder's Gazette,* V (April 17, 1884), 584.

28. Sam Webb, Albany, Texas, to C. C. Slaughter, Dallas, Texas, January 10, 1886, in Louis Hamilton Hill Papers (Southwest Collection, Texas Tech University, Lubbock).

29. Webb, Campbell, and Hill, Albany, Texas, to R. B. Mitchell, Troy, Penn[sylvania], January 31, 1887, in ibid.

30. Ibid.

31. Webb and Hill to Messrs. Mims and Sons, n.p., March 19, 1890, in ibid.

32. Webb, Campbell, and Hill to Geo[rge] W. West, Gainesville, Texas, July 8, 1886, in ibid.

33. Webb to L. W. Campbell, Waco, Texas, Nov[ember] 9, 1889, in ibid. For a more detailed analysis of this proposed railroad, see William Curry Holden, *Alkali Trails: Or Social and Economic Movements of the Texas Frontier, 1846–1900* (Dallas: The Southwest Press, 1930), 211–217.

34. Webb, Campbell, and Hill to Geo[rge] W. Hyreson, Dallas, Texas, July 8, 1886 (Hill Papers).

35. Quoted in Webb, Campbell, and Hill to Hyreson, December 13, 1886, in ibid.

36. Ibid.

37. Webb, Campbell, and Hill to Mrs. Mattie Haley, Erath Co[unty], Texas, June 13, 1887, in ibid.

38. Webb, Campbell, and Hill to Geo[rge] W. Collins, Trenton, K[entuck]y, August 11, 1887, in ibid.

39. Webb, Campbell, and Hill to J. C. Knox, Troy, Alabama, August 11, 1887, in ibid.

40. Webb to S. F. Look, Los Angeles, California, August 23, 1887, in ibid.

41. Webb, Campbell, and Hill to B. Scott, Columbia, Missouri, August 30, 1887, in ibid.

42. Webb, Campbell, and Hill to R. W. Connor, Fort Worth, Texas, July 6, 1888, in ibid.; Webb, Campbell, and Hill to John W. Taylor, [Louisville, Kentucky], September 21, 1888, in ibid.

43. After 1889, the firm abandoned the erratic practice of maintaining a separate set of letter press books for its cattle business. Thereafter, cattle-related correspondence is interspersed among the regular correspondence. See Hill Papers, passim.

44. U.S. Bureau of the Census, *Compendium of the Eleventh Census: 1890,* Pt. I, 399; *Texas Almanac: 1956–1957* (Dallas: A. H. Bello Corporation, 1956), 135. See also, Don Hamilton Biggers, *Shackelford County Sketches* (Albany, Texas: The Albany *News,* 1908), passim.

45. Sommerville to Mackay, Jan[uary] 1, 1884, Headquarters Division, Letters sent (Matador Records).

46. Vera Lea Dugas, "Texas Industry, 1860–1880," *Southwestern Historical Quarterly,* LIX (October, 1955), 159–169.

8

The National Trail Issue and the Decline of Trailing

1. Gard, "The Shawnee Trail," *Southwestern Historical Quarterly*, LVI, 363; *Laws of the State of Missouri Passed at the Eighteenth General Assembly, 1854–1855* (2 vols.; Jefferson City: James Lusk, Public Printer, 1855), II, 1104–1105; *General Laws of the Territory of Kansas Passed at the Fifth Session of the Legislative Assembly* (Lawrence: Herald of Freedom Press, 1859), 621–622.

2. *Laws of the State of Missouri Passed at the Regular Session of the 21st General Assembly* (Jefferson City: W. G. Cheeney, Public Printer, 1861), 25–28: "[A]ny constable or sheriff of the county . . . [shall] proceed without delay to remove such cattle condemned as a nuisance, driving said cattle as near as may be out of the state, or kill all of such cattle, if it shall be deemed necessary." *Ibid.*, 27; *General Laws of the State of Kansas Passed at the First Session of the Legislature, 1861* (Lawrence: Kansas State Journal, 1861), 279–281.

3. *The Laws of the State of Kansas Passed at the Sixth Session of the Legislature, 1866–1867* (2 vols. in one; Lawrence: Speer & Ross, 1866–1867), [I], 248.

4. Gard, *The Chisholm Trail*, 29–32; McCoy (Bieber, ed.), *Historic Sketches of the Cattle Trade*, 215–243; Samuel Lee Evans, "Texas Agriculture, 1880–1930" (Ph.D. dissertation, University of Texas at Austin, 1960), 320.

5. [Cox (ed.)], *Historical and Biographical Record of the Cattle Industry and the Cattlemen of Texas and Adjacent Territory*, 72.

6. McCoy (Bieber, ed.), *Historic Sketches of the Cattle Trade*, 223–229; U.S. Department of Agriculture, *Proceedings of a National Convention of Cattle Breeders and Others Called in Chicago, Illinois, November 15 and 16, 1883, by the Hon. Geo. B. Loving, Commissioner of Agriculture, to Consider the Subject of Contagious Diseases of Domestic Animals* (Washington: Government Printing Office, 1883), 19. See also, T. R. Havins, "Texas Fever," *Southwestern Historical Quarterly*, LII (July, 1948), 147–162, for a discussion of the disease and the attempts to control it.

7. John R. Mohler, *Texas or Tick Fever and Its Prevention* (Washington: Government Printing Office, 1906), 21.

8. McCoy (Bieber, ed.), *Historic Sketches of the Cattle Trade*, 252–255.

9. J. Evetts Haley, "Texas Fever and the Winchester Quarantine," *Panhandle-Plains Historical Review*, VIII (1935), 38–41; Holden, *Alkali Trails*, 39–40; Wilma Hixson, "The Influence of Water on the Settlement of the Llano Estacado" (M.A. thesis, West Texas State Teachers College, 1940), 49–50; Francis McNeill Alsup, "A History of the Panhandle of Texas" (M.A. thesis, University of Southern California, 1943), 108–110.

10. Ernest Staples Osgood, *The Day of the Cattleman* (Minneapolis: University of Minnesota Press, 1929), 165; Potter (Krehbiel, ed.), *Cattle*

Trails of the Old West, 20; Holden, *Alkali Trails,* 40–41; "Trail Driving," undated and unidentified MS, in Research File, Carl Coke Rister Papers (Southwest Collection, Texas Tech University, Lubbock).

11. *Laws of Kansas, 1866–1867,* [II], 263–276. See Thomas Donaldson, *The Public Domain* (Washington: Government Printing Office, 1884), 180. Although the 1867 line lay just a few miles west of Abilene, the area was underpopulated, and the law was not enforced. Gard, *The Chisholm Trail,* 65, incorrectly places the 1867 line some sixty miles west of Abilene. See also, *Laws of the State of Kansas Passed at the Twelfth Session of the Legislature* (Topeka: Commonwealth State Printing House, 1872), 387–390; *Session Laws of 1877* (Topeka: George W. Martin, 1877), 241; *The Session Laws of 1879* (Topeka: Geo. W. Martin, 1879), 345–346.

12. William C. Lamb, et al., Detroit, Kansas, to Gov[ernor S. J. Crawford], Topeka, Kansas, Aug[ust] 31, 1867, in Correspondence Received: Livestock, S. J. Crawford Papers (Archives, Kansas State Historical Society, Topeka).

13. H. H. Hawlett, Abilene, Kansas, to Sam[uel] J. Crawford, Nov[ember] 19, 1867, in ibid.

14. Representative of these demands are the following letters: M. Newton, Ellsworth, Kansas, to J. M. Harvey, Topeka, Feb[ruary] 3, 1869, in Letters Received: Livestock, J. M. Harvey Papers, in ibid.; R. G. Kessler, et al., Collyer, Kansas, to the Governor of Kansas, May 3, 1878, in Trego County Collection (Archives, Kansas State Historical Society, Topeka); S. Neill, Trego County, Kansas, to John St. John, Topeka, Feb[ruary] 13, 1880, in Letters Received: Livestock, John St. John Papers, in ibid.; E. P. Sheppard, Comanche County, Kansas, to St. John, April 20, 1880, in ibid.; H. D. Baner, Boonville, Kansas, to A. A. Holcomb, Topeka, August 4, 1884, in Letters Received: Livestock, G. W. Glick Papers, in ibid.

15. G. W. Glick, Governor's Proclamation, August 13, 1884, in Letters Received: Livestock (Glick Papers).

16. U.S. Congress, House, *Report No. 1228,* 49th Cong., 1st Sess. (1885–1886), contains information regarding cost differentials.

17. *The Breeder's Gazette,* VI (December 18, 1884), 900.

18. Groom to Brown, November 9, 1884, in "B. B. Groom" File (Francklyn Records). There is no clearly original source for the National Trail idea.

19. Sommerville to Mackay, Nov[ember] 14, 1884, in Letters sent, Headquarters Division (Matador Records).

20. Ford County (Kansas) *Globe,* January 29, 1884.

21. *The Breeder's Gazette,* V (April 17, 1884), 584.

22. A list of the delegates may be found in "Opening Session of the First National Cattle Growers' Convention," *Parson's Memorial and Historical Library Magazine,* I, 312–318. Three hundred and forty of the 719 delegates were Texans; many of the North Texans, however, did not support the National Trail issue. Ibid., passim. As far as can be determined, all delegates were seated without question. An example of delegate certification may be seen in O. W. Bill, President of the Kansas

State Short-Horn Breeders' Association, to whom it may concern, n.d., in J. L. McDowell Papers (Archives, Kansas State Historical Association, Topeka).

23. "Opening Session of the First National Cattle Growers' Convention," *Parson's Memorial and Historical Library Magazine*, I, 292.

24. Ibid.; *Proceedings of the First National Convention of Cattle Growers' of the United States Held at St. Louis, Mo., November 17th to 22d, 1884* (St. Louis: R. P. Studley & Co., 1884), 608.

25. "Opening Session of the First National Cattle Growers' Convention," *Parson's Memorial and Historical Library Magazine*, I, 296.

26. Ibid., 304.

27. Ibid., 304–305, 313–314. The contractors were: Seth Mabry and A. H. Pierce (Texas Live Stock Association); Thomas Dewees, G. W. West, D. R. Fant, J. M. Withers, J. H. Stephens, J. H. Presnall, J. A. Dewees, J. T. Lytle, and J. F. Ellison (Southern Texas Live Stock Association). Added to these were erstwhile drovers such as Eugene Millett of Kansas, Charles Goodnight and G. W. Littlefield of Texas, and R. D. Hunter and A. G. Evans of Missouri. All told, they comprised about 5 percent of the Texas delegation.

28. *Proceedings of the First National Convention of Cattle Growers'*, 76–77, 88–89.

29. Sommerville to Mackay, Nov[ember] 24, 1884, in Headquarters Division, Letters sent (Matador Records).

30. *The Breeder's Gazette*, VI (November 27, 1884), 778; ibid., VI (December 18, 1884), 900.

31. State of Kansas, "House Bill No. 116," undated copy in "B. B. Groom" File (Francklyn Records).

32. *Session Laws of 1885* (Topeka: Kansas Publishing House, 1885), 308–311.

33. John A. Martin, "Governor's Proclamation, State of Kansas," in Letters Received: Livestock, John A. Martin Papers (Archives, Kansas State Historical Society, Topeka). Although the governor called attention to 34° North latitude, the actual Kansas law drew the line at 37° North, or 30′ north of the Texas Panhandle. *Laws of Kansas, 1885*, pp. 309–310.

34. Nimmo, *Report on Range and Ranch Cattle Traffic*, 136–142, contains copies of the various quarantines as well as many of the arguments on either side of the quarantine and trail issues. See also, James A. Wilson, "West Texas Influence on the Early Cattle Industry of Arizona," *Southwestern Historical Quarterly*, LXXI (July, 1967), 32.

35. *Proceedings of the Third Annual Convention of Cattle Growers Held at Chicago, Ill., November 17 and 18, 1885* (Chicago: John Morris Company, 1886), 44ff.

36. Cattle Raisers' Association of Northwest Texas, "Minutes, [1877–1893]," March 10, 1885, in Texas and Southwestern Cattle Raisers Association Records (Archives, University of Texas at Austin).

37. [Texas, Governor], *Executive Series: Governor's Messages, Coke to Ross, 1874–1891* (Austin: Texas State Library, 1916), 515.

38. H. N. P. Gammel (comp.), *The Laws of Texas, 1822–1897* (10 vols.; Austin: The Gammel Book Company, 1898), IX, 745.
39. U.S. *Congressional Record*, 49th Cong., 1st Sess. (1885–1886), XVII, Pt. 1, 346, 376; Pt. 2, 2025; Pt. 3, 2521, 2573, 2668; Pt. 4, 3935–3936.
40. L. Q. C. Lamar, Department of the Interior, to S. J. R. McMillan, Senate of the United States, January 19, 1886, in Record Group 46 (National Archives).
41. U.S. *Congressional Record*, 49th Cong., 1st Sess. (1885–1886), XVII, Pt. 1, 346, 376; Pt. 2, 2025; Pt. 3, 2573, 2668; Pt. 4, 3935–3936.
42. U.S. Congress, House, *Executive Document No. 267*, 48th Cong., 2d Sess. (1884–1885); also published separately as Nimmo, *Report on Range and Ranch Cattle Traffic*, q.v.
43. Ibid., 39.
44. U.S. Congress, House, *Miscellaneous Document No. 36*, 48th Cong., 2d Sess. (1884–1885).
45. U.S. *Congressional Record*, 49th Cong., 1st Sess. (1885–1886), XVII, Pt. 1, 346, 376; Pt. 2, 2025; Pt. 3, 2521, 2573, 2668; Pt. 4, 3935–3936.
46. Sommerville to Mackay, Nov[ember] 25, [188]5, in Headquarters Division, Letters sent (Matador Records).
47. Ibid.
48. Stephens to Sommerville, March 1, 1885, in Headquarters Division, Letters received, in ibid.
49. Webb to J[o]hn T. Lytle, Lytle, Texas, January 12, 1886 (Hill Papers).
50. Webb to R. B. Mitchell, Troy P[ennsylvani]a, January 31, 1877, in ibid.; Cattle Raisers' Association of Northwest Texas, "Minutes," March [?], 1886 (Texas and Southwestern Cattle Raisers Association Records).
51. Sommerville to Stephens, Nov[ember] 25, 1885, in Headquarters Division, Letters sent (Matador Records).
52. Texas Live Stock Association, *Proceedings of the Fourth Annual Session* (Austin: Warner & Draughon, 1886), 27–28, 35.
53. Sommerville to Mackay, Dec[ember] 21, [188]5, in Headquarters Division, Letters sent (Matador Records); Texas Live Stock Association, *Proceedings of the Fourth Annual Session*, 35.
54. F. S. Reisdorph, "A History of the German People in the Texas Panhandle and Ellis County, Oklahoma" (M.A. thesis, West Texas State Teachers College, 1942), 37.
55. Lomax to B. F. Parks, n.p., July 7 [188]5, in Letters sent (Spur Records).
56. Lomax to C. M. Tilford, n.p., Apr[il] 29, [18]86, in ibid.; Lomax to N. W. Honea, Mouth of Duck [Creek, Texas], May 17, [18]86, in ibid.
57. Lomax to Cage, Ladd & Small, Kansas City, M[issour]i, July 5, [18]86, in ibid.
58. H. H. Campbell, Matador Land and Cattle Company, Ltd., to B. H. Campbell, [XIT Ranch], May 28, 1886, in "B. H. Campbell Correspondence File" (XIT Records).
59. [Las Vegas, New Mexico], *The Stock Grower*, July 6, 1887.
60. U.S. Congress, Senate, *Executive Document No. 24*, 51st Cong., 1st Sess. (1889–1890), 8–9.

61. John Sayles and Henry Sayles, *Sayles' Annotated Civil Statutes* (2 vols.; St. Louis: The Gilbert Book Company, 1897), II, 1751–1753; Fort Worth *Star-Telegram*, October 30, 1949; Evans, "Texas Agriculture, 1880–1930," 231–232.

Bibliography

THIS BIBLIOGRAPHY is divided into two sections: "Manuscript Collections" and "Theses, Dissertations, and Printed Works." The individual, unpublished documents cited in the footnotes are described in such a way as to facilitate their location within larger bodies of manuscript material. For that reason, whole manuscript collections, such as the Records of the Matador Land and Cattle Company, Ltd., and not the numerous, specific letters used from that collection, are the units listed in the bibliography. The several documents (letters and interviews) collected by the author in the process of researching this work are grouped together under Skaggs Papers.

The latter category, as is the former, is arranged alphabetically by main entry and is keyed to the footnote citations. Both are limited to works cited.

Manuscript Collections

Card, Lottie Holman. Papers. Southwest Collection, Texas Tech University.

Cattle Raisers' Association of Northwest Texas. Records (in Texas and Southwestern Cattle Raisers Association, Records). Archives, University of Texas at Austin.

Coggin Brothers and Associates. Records. Southwest Collection, Texas Tech University.

Collinson, Frank. Papers. Southwest Collection, Texas Tech University.

Francklyn Land and Cattle Company. Records. Archives, Panhandle-Plains Historical Museum, Canyon, Texas.

Franks, Johnny. Interview. April 1, 1967. Oral History File, Southwest Collection, Texas Tech University.

Glick, G. W. Papers. Archives, Kansas State Historical Society, Topeka.

Hamlin, James D. Papers. Southwest Collection, Texas Tech University.

Harvey, James D. Papers. Archives, Kansas State Historical Society, Topeka.

Hill, Louis Hamilton. Papers. Southwest Collection, Texas Tech University.

Lytle, Leonard. "Outline of the Lytle Families of America," 1932. Cincinnati, Ohio, Public Library.

McDowell, J. L. Papers. Kansas State Historical Society, Topeka.

Martin, John A. Papers. Archives, Kansas State Historical Society, Topeka.

Matador Land and Cattle Company, Ltd. Records. Southwest Collection, Texas Tech University.

Pryor, Ike T. Papers. Archives, University of Texas at Austin.

Rister, Carl Coke. Papers. Southwest Collection, Texas Tech University.
Skaggs, Jimmy M. Papers. Possession of the author.
Spur Ranch. Records. Southwest Collection, Texas Tech University.
St. John, John. Papers. Archives, Kansas State Historical Society, Topeka.
Streeter, Floyd Benjamin. Papers. Special Collections, Ablah Library, Wichita State University.
Trego County. Collection. Archives, Kansas State Historical Society, Topeka.
United States. Department of the Army. Records (Record Groups 94 and 98). National Archives, Washington, D.C.
United States. Department of the Interior. Records (Record Group 46). National Archives, Washington, D.C.
United States. War Department Collection of Confederate Records (Record Group 109). National Archives, Washington, D.C.
VanDale, Earl. Papers. Archives, University of Texas at Austin.
XIT Ranch. Records. Archives, Panhandle-Plains Historical Museum, Canyon, Texas.

Theses, Dissertations, and Printed Works

Abbott, E. C. "John R. Blocker, King of the Texas Trail," *Frontier Times,* 14 (August, 1937), 497–498.

———— and Helena Huntington Smith, *We Pointed Them North: Recollections of a Cowpuncher.* New York: Farrar & Rinehart, Inc., 1939.

Adams, Andy. *Reed Anthony, Cowman: An Autobiography.* Boston: Houghton Mifflin Company, 1907.

"Alonzo Millett," in Hunter, *Trail Drivers of Texas,* q.v.

Alsup, Frances McNeill. "A History of the Panhandle of Texas." M.A. thesis, University of Southern California, 1943.

Anderson, L. B. "A Few Thrilling Incidents in My Experiences on the Trail," in Hunter, *Trail Drivers of Texas,* q.v.

————. "Habits and Customs of Early Texans," in Hunter, *Trail Drivers of Texas,* q.v.

Atherton, Lewis. *The Cattle Kings.* Bloomington: Indiana University Press, 1961.

Bennett, Bob. *Kerr County, Texas: 1856–1956.* San Antonio: The Naylor Company, 1956.

Biggers, Don Hamilton. *Shackelford County Sketches.* Albany, Texas: The Albany *News,* 1908.

Black, A. P. *The End of the Long Horn Trail.* N.p.: n.p., n.d.

Black, Gus. "Had Plenty of Fun," in Hunter, *Trail Drivers of Texas,* q.v.

[Blocker, Abner P.]. "Ab Blocker Tells about Trail Driving Days," in Hunter, *Trail Drivers of Texas,* q.v.

————. "The Man Who Had Hell in His Neck," in Hunter, *Trail Drivers of Texas,* q.v.

————. "The Trail Drivers of Texas," in Hunter, *Trail Drivers of Texas,* q.v.

152

Borroum, B. A. "Recollections of Old Trail Days," in Hunter, *Trail Drivers of Texas*, q.v.

Breeder's Gazette, The. V-VI.

Brown, Dee and Martin F. Schmitt. *Trail Driving Days.* New York: Charles Scribner's Sons, 1952.

Brayer, Garnet M. and Herbert O. Brayer. *American Cattle Trails.* New York: Western Range Cattle Industry Study, 1952.

Byler, J. M. "Got 'Wild and Woolly' on the Chisholm Trail," in Hunter, *Trail Drivers of Texas*, q.v.

"Captain Charles Schreiner," in Hunter, *Trail Drivers of Texas*, q.v.

Carson, G. M. "When Ab Blocker Climbed a Fence," in Hunter, *Trail Drivers of Texas*, q.v.

Cauley, T. J. "Early Business Methods in the Texas Cattle Industry," *Journal of Economics and Business*, 4 (May, 1932), 29–38.

Chapman, Joe. "An Old Frontiersman Tells His Experiences," in Hunter, *Trail Drivers of Texas*, q.v.

Chrisman, Harry E. *Lost Trails of the Cimarron.* Denver. Sage Books, 1964.

Clark, J. Stanley. "Texas Fever in Oklahoma," *Chronicles of Oklahoma*, 29 (Winter, 1951–1952), 429–443.

Clark, L. T. "Worked for George W. Saunders," in Hunter, *Trail Drivers of Texas*, q.v.

Clay, John. *My Life on the Plains.* 2d ed.; New York: Antiquarian Press, 1961.

Clemen, Rudolph A. "The Meat Packing Industry in the United States." Ph.D. dissertation, Harvard University, 1921.

Collinson, Frank (Mary Whatley Clarke, ed.). *Life in the Saddle.* Norman: University of Oklahoma Press, 1963.

"Colonel Dillard R. Fant," in Hunter, *Trail Drivers of Texas*, q.v.

Connolly, Jeff. "Hit the Trail in High Places," in Hunter, *Trail Drivers of Texas*, q.v.

[Cox, James (ed.)]. *Historical and Biographical Record of the Cattle Industry and Cattlemen of Texas and Adjacent Territory.* St. Louis: Woodard & Tiernan Printing Co., 1895.

Cox, M. L. "Fort Griffin—Cowtown!" *The Cattleman*, 50 (March, 1964), 61, 83.

Craig, Hiram C. "Days Gone By," in Hunter, *Trail Drivers of Texas*, q.v.

Crawford, F. G. "Drove Horses to Mississippi," in Hunter, *Trail Drivers of Texas*, q.v.

Custer, J.M. "Scouting and Routing in the Good Old Days," in Hunter, *Trail Drivers of Texas*, q.v.

Dale, Edward Everett. *Cow Country.* Norman: University of Oklahoma Press, 1942.

———. *The Range Cattle Industry: Ranching on the Great Plains from 1865 to 1925.* Norman: University of Oklahoma Press, 1930.

Dallas Morning News. November 18, 1886; January 11, 1907; September 25, 1937.

"David C. Pryor," in Hunter, *Trail Drivers of Texas*, q.v.

Davis, Ellis A. and Edwin H. Grobe (comp. and eds.). *The New Encyclopedia of Texas* (5 vols.). Dallas: Texas Development Bureau, [1929].

Doan, Corwin. "Reminiscences of the Trail," in Hunter, *Trail Drivers of Texas*, q.v.

Dobie, J. Frank. "Ab Blocker: Trail Boss," *Arizona and the West*, 6 (Summer, 1964), 97–103.

———. "George W. Saunders, My Friend," *Frontier Times*, 10 (August, 1933), 538–541.

———. "Hunting Cousin Salley," *Southwest Review*, 43 (Summer, 1963), 177–188.

———. *The Longhorns*. New York: Little, Brown and Company, 1941.

[Dodge City]. *Ford County Globe*. April 17, July 1, 1884.

Donaldson, Thomas. *The Public Domain*. Washington: Government Printing Office, 1884.

Douglas, C. L. *Cattle Kings of Texas*. Dallas: Cecil Baugh, 1939.

Drago, Harry Sinclair. *Great American Cattle Trails*. New York: Dodd, Mead & Company, 1965.

Dugas, Vera Lea. "Texas Industry, 1860–1880," *Southwestern Historical Quarterly*, 59 (October, 1955), 151–183.

Durham, Philip and Everett L. Jones. *The Negro Cowboy*. New York: Dodd, Mead & Company, 1965.

Dykstra, Robert R. *The Cattle Towns*. New York: Alfred A. Knopf, 1968.

Elliott, Claude. "Union Sentiment in Texas, 1861–1865," *Southwestern Historical Quarterly*, 50 (April, 1947), 315–328.

Ellison, J. F., Jr. "Made Several Trips up the Trail," in Hunter, *Trail Drivers of Texas*, q.v.

———. "Sketch of Colonel J. F. Ellison," in Hunter, *Trail Drivers of Texas*, q.v.

———. "Traveling the Trail with Good Men Was a Pleasure," in Hunter, *Trail Drivers of Texas*, q.v.

Ellsworth [Kansas] *Messenger*. February 3, 10, 17, 24, March 2, 9, 16, 1916.

Emmett, Chris. *Shanghai Pierce: A Fair Likeness*. Norman: University of Oklahoma Press, 1953.

Erwin, Alan A. *The Southwest of John B. Slaughter, 1841–1922: Pioneer Cattleman and Trail-Driver of Texas, the Pecos, and Arizona*. Glendale: The Arthur H. Clark Company, 1965.

Evans, Samuel Lee. "Texas Agriculture, 1880–1930." Ph.D. dissertation, University of Texas at Austin, 1960.

Fielder, W. F. "When the Elements Wept and Shed Tears," in Hunter, *Trail Drivers of Texas*, q.v.

Ford, Gus (ed.). *Texas Cattle Brands*. Dallas: Clyde C. Cockrell Company, 1936.

[Ford, Henry]. "Coggin & Bro.," in [Cox (ed.)], *Historical and Biographical Record of the Cattle Industry*, q.v.

Fort Griffin *Echo*. May 21, 1879.

Fort Worth *Democrat*. April 24, 1875.

Fort Worth *Star-Telegram*. October 30, 1949.

[Freeman, James W. (ed.)]. *Prose and Poetry of the Live Stock Industry of the United States.* Kansas City, Mo.: Hudson-Kimberly Company, 1904.

French, C. C. "When the Temperature Was 72 Below Zero," in Hunter, *Trail Drivers of Texas,* q.v.

Gammel, H. N. P. (comp.). *The Laws of Texas, 1822–1897* (10 vols.). Austin: The Gammel Book Company, 1898.

Gard, Wayne. *The Chisholm Trail.* Norman: University of Oklahoma Press, 1954.

———. "The Impact of the Cattle Trails," *Southwestern Historical Quarterly,* 71 (July, 1967), 1–6.

———. "Retracing the Chisholm Trail," *Southwestern Historical Quarterly,* 60 (July, 1956), 51–68.

———. "The Shawnee Trail," *Southwestern Historical Quarterly,* 56 (January, 1953), 359–377.

Garner, James Marion. "Some Trips up the Trail," in Hunter, *Trail Drivers of Texas,* q.v.

Garner, Sam. "Paid Three Dollars for Five Gallons of Water," in Hunter, *Trail Drivers of Texas,* q.v.

Gentry, Mary Jane. "Thurber: The Life and Death of a Texas Town." M.A. thesis, University of Texas at Austin, 1946.

"George W. West," in Hunter, *Trail Drivers of Texas,* q.v.

Goodnight, Charles. "The Killing of Oliver Loving," in Hunter, *Trail Drivers of Texas,* q.v.

———. "More About the Chisholm Trail," in Hunter, *Trail Drivers of Texas,* q.v.

Gracy, David B., II. "George Washington Littlefield: Portrait of a Cattleman," *Southwestern Historical Quarterly,* 68 (October, 1964), 237–258.

———. *Littlefield Lands: Colonization on the Texas Plains, 1912–1920.* Austin: University of Texas Press, 1968.

Grant, Ben O. "The Early History of Shackelford County." M.A. thesis, Hardin-Simmons University, 1936.

———. "Life in Old Fort Griffin," *West Texas Historical Association Year Book,* 10 (October, 1934), 32–41.

Gressley, Gene M. *Bankers and Cattlemen.* New York: Alfred A. Knopf, 1966.

Guide Map of the Great Texas Cattle Trail from Red River Crossing to the Old Reliable Kansas Pacific Railroad. N.p.: Kansas Pacific Railroad, 1875.

Haley, J. Evetts. *Charles Goodnight, Cowman & Plainsman.* Boston: Houghton, Mifflin Company, 1936.

———. *Charles Schreiner, General Merchandise: The Story of a Country Store.* Austin: Texas State Historical Association, 1944.

———. *George W. Littlefield, Texan.* Norman: University of Oklahoma Press, 1943.

———. "A Survey of Texas Cattle Drives to the North, 1866–1895." M.A. thesis, University of Texas at Austin, 1926.

155

————. "Texas Fever and the Winchester Quarantine," *Panhandle-Plains Historical Review*, 8 (1935), 37–53.

————. *The XIT Ranch of Texas and the Early Days of the Llano Estacado*. Chicago: The Lakeside Press, 1929.

Handins, J. M. "Reminiscences of Old Trail Driving," in Hunter, *Trail Drivers of Texas*, q.v.

Hardman, W. B. "Tells about Bob Robertson," in Hunter, *Trail Drivers of Texas*, q.v.

Hart, Peter. *Description of Shackelford County, State of Texas, U.S.A.: Its Creation, Organization, Wealth, and Productiveness, with a Synopsis of Its Soil, Climate, Products, Etc.* Albany, Texas: Shackelford County, 1886.

Harvey, T. Fred. "George Findlay, General Manager of the XIT Ranch, 1888–1889." M.A. thesis, West Texas State College, 1950.

Havins, T. R. "Texas Fever," *Southwestern Historical Quarterly*, 52 (October, 1948), 147–162.

Hawkins, T. T. "When George Saunders Made a Bluff Stick," in Hunter, *Trail Drivers of Texas*, q.v.

Hill, J. L. *The End of the Cattle Trail*. Long Beach: Geo. W. Moyle Printing Co., [1923].

History of the Cattlemen of Texas: A Brief Resume of the Live Stock Industry of the Southwest and a Biographical Sketch of the Important Characters Whose Lives are Interwoven Therein. Dallas: The Johnson Printing and Advertising Co., 1914.

Hixson, Wilma. "The Influence of Water upon the Settlement of the Llano Estacado." M.A. thesis, West Texas State Teachers College, 1940.

Holden, William Curry. *Alkali Trails: Or, Social and Economic Movements of the Texas Frontier, 1846–1900*. Dallas: The Southwestern Press, 1930.

Hollon, Gene. "Captain Charles Schreiner, the Father of the Hill Country," *Southwestern Historical Quarterly*, 43 (October, 1944), 145–168.

Houston, Samuel Dunn. "A Trying Trip Alone through the Wilderness," in Hunter, *Trail Drivers of Texas*, q.v.

Humphries, J. R. "From the Nueces to the North Platte," in Hunter, *Trail Drivers of Texas*, q.v.

Hunter, J. Marvin. "Ab Blocker and the XIT," *Frontier Times*, XXI (October, 1943), 42–44.

————. "George Saunders' First Trip," *Frontier Times*, V (May, 1928), 321–324.

————. "Ike T. Pryor Was a Great Cattleman," *Frontier Times*, 26 (October, 1948), 129–131.

————. *The Story of Lottie Deno: Her Life and Times*. Bandera, Texas: The 4 Hunters, 1959.

———— (comp. amd ed.). *The Trail Drivers of Texas* (2 vols.). N.p.: n.p., 1920. Rev. Vol. I; N.p.: n.p., 1924. Comb. ed.; Nashville: Cokesbury Press, 1925.

Jackman, W. T. "Where They Put a Trail Boss in Jail," in Hunter, *Trail Drivers of Texas*, q.v.

156

Jennings, R. J. "Cowboys Dressed Up at the End of the Trail," in Hunter, *Trail Drivers of Texas*, q.v.

"John T. Lytle," in Hunter, *Trail Drivers of Texas*, q.v.

Johnson, C. E. "Could Ride a Hundred Miles in a Day," in Hunter, *Trail Drivers of Texas*, q.v.

[Jones, Jack], as told to Ruth Hunnicutt. "Plain Talk from Jack Jones," *The Cattleman*, 32 (October, 1945), 131–133.

Kansas City *Star*. July 27, 1908.

[Kansas. Laws, statutes, etc.]. *General Laws of the State of Kansas Passed at the First Session of the Legislature, 1861*. Lawrence: Kansas State Journal, 1861.

————. *Laws of the State of Kansas Passed at the Sixth Session of the Legislature, 1866–1867* (2 vols. in one). Lawrence: Speer & Ross, 1867.

————. *Laws of the State of Kansas Passed at the Twelfth Session of the Legislature*. Topeka: Commonwealth State Printing House, 1872.

————. *Laws of the Territory of Kansas Passed at the Fifth Session of the Legislative Assembly*. Lawrence: Herald of Freedom Streams Press, 1859.

————. *Session Laws of 1877*. Topeka: George W. Martin, 1877.

————. *Session Laws of 1879*. Topeka: Geo. W. Martin, 1879.

————. *Session Laws of 1885*. Topeka: Kansas Publishing House, 1885.

Kritzer, John S. "Lost Twenty-One Thousand Dollars on One Drive," in Hunter, *Trail Drivers of Texas*, q.v.

[Las Vegas, New Mexico]. *The Stock Grower*. July 16, 1887.

Lauderdale, Jasper. "Reminiscences of the Trail," in Hunter, *Trail Drivers of Texas*, q.v.

Love, Clara M. "History of the Cattle Industry in the Southwest," *Southwestern Historical Quarterly*, 19 (April, 1916), 370–399; 20 (July, 1916), 1–18.

Lynch, Vernon. "1879 in the *Echo*: A Year at Fort Griffin on the Texas Frontier," West Texas Historical Association *Year Book*, 41 (October, 1965), 51–79.

McArthur, Daniel Evander. "The Cattle Industry of Texas, 1685–1918." M.A. thesis, University of Texas at Austin, 1918.

McCaleb, J. L. "My First Five-Dollar Bill," in Hunter, *Trail Drivers of Texas*, q.v.

McCoy, Joseph G. (Ralph P. Bieber, ed.). *Historic Sketches of the Cattle Trade of the West and Southwest*. Glendale: The Arthur H. Clark Company, 1940.

Miller, Nyle H. and Joseph W. Snell. *Great Gunfighters of the Kansas Cowtowns, 1867–1886*. Lincoln: University of Nebraska Press, 1963.

Mills, G. M. "Experiences 'Tenderfeet' Could Not Survive," in Hunter, *Trail Drivers of Texas*, q.v.

[Missouri. Laws, statutes, etc.]. *Laws of Missouri Passed at the Eighteenth General Assembly, 1854–1855* (2 vols.). Jefferson City: James Lusk, 1855.

157

————. *Laws of the State of Missouri Passed at the Regular Session of the 21st General Assembly.* Jefferson City: W. G. Cheeney, 1861.

Mitchell, Glynn. "History of Coleman County." M.A. thesis, University of Texas at Austin, 1949.

Mohler, John R. *Texas or Tick Fever and Its Prevention.* Washington: Government Printing Office, 1906.

Mooar, J. Wright. "Frontier Experiences of J. Wright Mooar," West Texas Historical Association *Year Book*, 4 (June, 1928), 89–92.

Moore, Bonnie Cathryn. "The Northern Drives of Texas after 1866." M.A. thesis, University of Oklahoma, 1934.

Myres, John Myres. *Doc Holliday.* Boston: Little, Brown and Company, 1955.

Neill, Sam. "A Long Time Between Drinks," in Hunter, *Trail Drivers of Texas*, q.v.

Newman, Ruth G. "The Industrialization of Fort Worth." M.S. thesis, North Texas State College, 1950.

Nimmo, Joseph. *Report of the Chief of the Bureau of Statistics on Range and Ranch Cattle Traffic.* Washington: Government Printing Office, 1885. See also, U.S. Congress, House. *Executive Document No. 267,* q.v.

Nye, W. S. *Carbine and Lance: The Story of Old Fort Sill.* Norman: University of Okalhoma Press, 1937.

"One of the Best Known Trail Drivers," in Hunter, *Trail Drivers of Texas,* q.v.

"Opening Session of the First National Cattle Growers' Convention," *Parson's Memorial and Historical Library Magazine,* I (1885), 290–330.

Osgood, Ernest Staples. *The Day of the Cattleman.* Minneapolis: University of Minnesota Press, 1929.

Padgitt, James T. "Early Days in Coleman County," West Texas Historical Association *Year Book*, 28 (October, 1952), 81–86.

Pierce, Bessie Louise. *A History of Chicago* (3 vols.). New York: Alfred A. Knopf, 1937–1957.

Polk, F. M. "My Experiences on the Cow Trail," in Hunter, *Trail Drivers of Texas*, q.v.

Potter, Jack (Laura R. Krehbiel, ed.). *Cattle Trails of the Old West.* Clayton, N.M.: Laura R. Krehbiel, 1939.

Powell, Cutbert. *Twenty Years of Kansas City's Live Stock Trade and Traders.* Kansas City: Pearl Printing Company, 1893.

Proceedings of the First National Convention of Cattle Growers' of the United States Held at St. Louis, Mo., November 17th to 22d, 1884. St. Louis: R. P. Studley & Co., 1884.

Proceedings of the Third Annual Convention of Cattle Growers Held at Chicago, Ill., November 17 and 18, 1885. Chicago: John Morris Company, 1886.

Pryor, Ike T. "The Cost of Moving a Herd to Northern Markets," in Hunter, *Trail Drivers of Texas*, q.v.

————. "The Remarkable Career of Colonel Ike T. Pryor," in Hunter, *Trail Drivers of Texas*, q.v.

Reisdorph, F. S. "A History of the German People in the Texas Panhandle and Ellis County, Oklahoma." M.A. thesis, West Texas State Teachers College, 1942.

"R. G. (Dick) Head," in Hunter, *Trail Drivers of Texas*, q.v.

Riding, Sam P. *The Chisholm Trail*. Guthrie, Okla.: Co-operative Publishing Company, 1933.

Rogers, Jerry L. "'The Indian Territory Expedition' of Colonel Nelson Appleton Miles." M.A. thesis, Texas Technological College, 1965.

San Angelo *Standard Times*. August 29, 1954.

San Antonio *Daily Light*. January 11, 1907.

Saunders, George W. "John and Thomas Dewees," in Hunter, *Trail Drivers of Texas*, q.v.

––––––. "Origins and Close of the Old-Time Northern Trail," in Hunter, *Trail Drivers of Texas*, q.v.

––––––. "Reflections of the Trail," in Hunter, *Trail Drivers of Texas*, q.v.

––––––. "Shanghai Pierce," in Hunter, *Trail Drivers of Texas*, q.v.

Saunders, W. D. H. "Drove a Herd to Mississippi and Alabama," in Hunter, *Trail Drivers of Texas*, q.v.

Sayles, John and Henry Sayles. *Sayles' Annotated Civil Statutes* (2 vols.). Austin: The Gilbert Book Company, 1897.

"Seth Mabry," in Hunter, *Trail Drivers of Texas*, q.v.

Sheffy, Lester Field. *The Francklyn Land and Cattle Company: A Panhandle Enterprise, 1882–1957*. Austin: Texas State Historical Association, 1964.

Shefrin, Jack Allen. "The Chisholm Trail." M.A. thesis, University of Kansas City, 1940.

Skaggs, Jimmy M. "The Economic Impact of Trailing: One Aspect," West Texas Historical Association *Year Book*, 58 (October, 1967), 18–30.

––––––. "Frontier Business Diversifications: The Webb and Hill Company of Albany, Texas," West Texas Historical Association *Year Book*, 64 (October, 1968), 26–36.

––––––. "The Great Western Cattle Trail to Dodge City, Kansas." M.A. thesis, Texas Technological College, 1965.

––––––. "Hip Pocket Businessmen: The Cattle-Trailing Contractors," *Great Plains Journal*, 10 (Fall, 1970), 1–10.

––––––. "John Thomas Lytle: Cattle Baron," *Southwestern Historical Quarterly*, 71 (July, 1967), 46–60.

––––––. "The National Trail Issue and the Decline of Cattle Trailing," *The Museum Journal*, 11 (1969), 1–24.

––––––. "A Study in Business Failure: Frank Collinson in the Big Bend," *Panhandle-Plains Historical Review*, 43 (1970), 9–20.

"Sketch of Colonel J. J. Myres," in Hunter, *Trail Drivers of Texas*, q.v.

"Sketch of J. M. Choate," in Hunter, *Trail Drivers of Texas*, q.v.

"Sketch of L. B. Allen," in Hunter, *Trail Drivers of Texas*, q.v.

[Slaughter, W. B.?]. "George Webb Slaughter," in Hunter, *Trail Drivers of Texas*, q.v.

Smith, Joe P. "Made Several Trips," in Hunter, *Trail Drivers of Texas*, q.v.

Spode, Robert William. "W. W. Johnson and Beginnings of Coal Mining in

159

the Strawn-Thurber Vicinity, 1880–1888," West Texas Historical Association *Year Book*, 44 (October, 1968), 48–59.

Storey, E. M. "Got Their Names in the Pot for Supper and Breakfast," in Hunter, *Trail Drivers of Texas*, q.v.

Stout, Faun Vernon. "The History and Development of Education in Wilbarger County from 1858 to 1937." M.A. thesis, Southern Methodist University, 1937.

[Texas. Governor]. *Executive Series: Governor's Messages, Coke to Ross, 1874–1891.* Austin: Texas State Library, 1916.

[Texas. Laws, statutes, etc.]. See: Gammel, *The Laws of Texas*, and Sayles and Sayles, *Sayles' Annotated Civil Statutes*, q.q.v.

Texas Almanac, 1956–1957. Dallas: A. H. Bello Corporation, 1956.

"Texas Collection," *Southwestern Historical Quarterly*, 44 (July, 1940), 117–133.

Texas Live Stock Association. *Proceedings of the Fourth Annual Session.* Austin: Warner & Draughon, 1886.

Texas State Gazetteer and Business Directory, 1892 (4 vols.). Detroit: R. L. Polk & Co., 1892.

"Thomas Jefferson Moore," in Hunter, *Trail Drivers of Texas*, q.v.

Thompson, Oscar. "Were Happier in the Good Old Days," in Hunter, *Trail Drivers of Texas*, q.v.

———. "My Trip Up the Trail," in Hunter, *Trail Drivers of Texas*, q.v.

Tinkler, Estelle D. "Nobility's Ranche: A History of the Rocking Ranche," *Panhandle-Plains Historical Review*, 15 (1942), 1–96.

Tucker, Leo. "Kidnapped the Inspectors," in Hunter, *Trail Drivers of Texas*, q.v.

U.S. Bureau of the Census. *Compendium of the Eleventh Census: 1890.* Washington: Government Printing Office, 1892.

———. *Statistics of the Population of the United States at the Ninth Census.* Washington: Government Printing Office, 1873.

———. *Statistics of the Population of the United States at the Tenth Census.* Washington: Government Printing Office, 1883.

U.S. Congress. House. *Executive Document No. 267.* 48th Cong., 2d Sess. (1884–1885). See also, Nimmo, *Report on Range and Ranch Cattle Traffic*, q.v.

———. *Miscellaneous Document No. 36.* 48th Cong., 2d Sess. (1884–1885).

———. *Report No. 1228.* 49th Cong., 1st Sess. (1885–1886).

U.S. Congress. Senate *Executive Document No. 14.* 49th Cong., 1st Sess. (1885–1886).

———. *Executive Document No. 24.* 51st Cong., 1st. Sess. (1889–1890).

U.S. *Congressional Record.* Vol. X, XVII.

U.S. Department of Agriculture. *Proceedings of a National Convention of Cattle Breeders and Others Called in Chicago, Illinois, November 15 and 16, 1883, by the Hon. Geo. B. Loving, Commissioner of Agriculture, to Consider the Subject of Contagious Diseases in Domestic Animals.* Washington: Government Printing Office, 1883.

Wallace, Ernest. *Ranald S. Mackenzie on the Texas Frontier.* Lubbock: West Texas Museum Association, 1964.

Webb, Walter Prescott and H. Bailey Carroll (eds.). *The Handbooks of Texas* (2 vols.). Austin: Texas State Historical Association, 1952.

Welder, Thomas. "Preferred to Take Older Cattle up the Trail," in Hunter, *Trail Drivers of Texas,* q.v.

Wells, John. "Met Quanah Parker on the Trail," in Hunter, *Trail Drivers of Texas,* q.v.

[West, Sol]. "Courage and Hardihood on the Old Texas Cattle Trail," in Hunter, *Trail Drivers of Texas,* q.v.

"William G. Butler," in Hunter, *Trail Drivers of Texas,* q.v.

Williams, H. C. "Took Time to Visit His Sweetheart," in Hunter, *Trail Drivers of Texas,* q.v.

"William Henry Jennings," in Hunter, *Trail Drivers of Texas,* q.v.

"William Henry Jennings," in *History of the Cattleman of Texas,* q.v.

Wilson, James A. "West Texas Influence on the Early Cattle Industry of Arizona," *Southwestern Historical Quarterly,* 71 (July, 1967), 26–36.

Withers, Richard. "The Experiences of an Old Trail Driver," in Hunter, *Trail Drivers of Texas,* q.v.

"W. M. Choate," in Hunter, *Trail Drivers of Texas,* q.v.

Word, N. L. "Made Several Trips up the Trail," in Hunter, *Trail Drivers of Texas,* q.v.

Wright, Robert M. *Dodge City, the Cowboy Capital, and the Great Southwest.* [Wichita: Wichita *Eagle* Press, 1913].

———. "Early Days in Dodge City," *Frontier Times,* 26 (September, 1949), 317–322.

Index

General topics that appear on virtually every page of this book—such as cattle, Texas, and cowboys—have not been indexed.

136 (n. 29); business methods of, 45–47, 50; cattle drives by, 45, 47–50; employee relations of, 49–50; organization of, 44, 46; Texas fever and, 48, 51; volume of business of, 47, 49–51, 136 (n. 29)
Boophilus bovis, 22, 102–121
bordellos, *see* prostitution
Borroum, B. A., 139 (n. 10)
Borroum, James, 61, 139 (n. 10)
Bosler, George, 38
Bosler, J. W., 38
Bosque Grande, N. M., 5–6
Bowie, James, 27–28
Brackettville, Tex., 14
Brady, Tex., 54
Breeders' Gazette (periodical), 113–114
Brewster County, Tex., 44
Brookville, Kan., 88
Brown, Frank G., 22, 109
Brown County, Tex., 4, 41–44
Brownwood, Tex., 44
Buel, M. P., 83
buffalo hunters, 92, 94
Buffalo Springs, Tex., 47–48
Bunker Hill, Ill., 78
Bureau of Animal Industry, *see* U.S. Bureau of Animal Industry
Burnett, Samuel Burk, 13
Byler, James, 67

Cain, Bill, 52
Cairo, Ill., 31
Caldwell County, Tex., 62
California, 28, 33, 81
Campbell, B. H., 47, 51
Campbell, H. H., 2
Campbell, L. W., 95, 97; *see also* Webb, Campbell, and Hill Land and Cattle Company
Camp Supply, I.T., 48
Canada, 96, 109, 114; quarantine by, 114
Capitol Freehold Land and Investment Company, *see* XIT Ranch
Carlotta, Mex., 4
Carson, G. M., 49
Cassidy Commission Company, *see*

Scruggs and Cassidy Commission Company
Castroville, Tex., 15
cattle buyers, 4, 73–86; *see also* commission agencies, and U.S. government
cattle contractors, *see* transportation agencies
cattle dipping, 121
cattle drives, 1–10, 15, 17–19, 23, 30–35, 38, 42–44, 48–49, 51–56, 60, 62, 64–67, 70–71, 81, 87–88, 96–99, 119–121, 123; cost of, 1–3, 54–55, 88, 108; decline of, 23, 51, 56, 96–99, 119–121; Indians and, 8, 17–18, 42–43, 60, 88; losses by, 3, 7–8, 54–55; military aid and, 17–18, 93; organization of, 9; problems of, 31, 54, 78–79; profits from, 3, 5–6; ranching and, 2–3, 5, 9–10; thefts by, 8, 55, 123; volume of, 123; to Arizona, 70; to Colorado, 6, 44, 53, 56; to Dakota Territory, 3, 7, 34, 51, 55; to Idaho, 35; to Illinois, 31; to Indian Territory, 3; to Iowa, 62; to Kansas, 2–5, 17, 19, 31–33, 35, 42, 48–49, 52, 55, 60, 64–67, 71, 81, 87; to Louisiana, 30, 67; to Missouri, 30–31; to Mexico, 67; to Montana, 3, 7, 55; to Nebraska, 17, 19, 53, 64; to Nevada, 32–33; to New Mexico, 4–5, 43–44; to Texas, 38, 44; to Utah, 62; to Wyoming, 3, 6, 50, 55, 64
Cattle Kings' (Cattle Trail) Railroad, 97
cattle markets, 14, 33, 73–86
cattle prices, 4, 7, 15, 35–37, 45, 49–50, 60, 96–97, 117–118
Cattle Raisers Association of Northwest Texas, *see* Northwest Texas Cattle Raisers Association
cattle ticks, *see Boophilus bovis*
cattle towns, *see* trail towns
cattle trails, 5, 15, 17–18, 33, 35, 43, 87–101, 103–123; community growth and, 87–101; *see also*

164

60; *see also* Dewees, Ervin, and Ellison Cattle Company

Ellison, Bishop, and Dewees Cattle Company, 61

Ellison and Dewees Cattle Company, 59–62

Ellsworth, Kan., 3, 35–36, 80, 88–89, 107

El Paso, Tex., 82

employment, 85, 89, 100

English, ranching investments by, 25

Erath County, Tex., 83

Evans, Albert G., 80–84, 148 (n. 27); *see also* Hunter, Evans and Company, and Patterson, Evans and Company

Evans, Snider & Buel Commission Company, Inc., 83

Evansville, Ark., 80–81

Ewing, Alexander, 30

Ewing, E. A., 111

Ewing, Mrs. John O., 52

F (brand), 64

Faltin, August, 16

Fant, Dillard Rucker, 3–4, 63–65, 68, 71, 148 (n. 27); volume of business of, 64

Fant, Mary (Burriss), 63

Fant, W. N., 63

farmers, 17, 31, 41, 45, 52, 59–60, 70, 93, 96, 103, 112, 125

Farr, Jeff, 54–55

Fawcett, Harry, 69

Federal government, *see* U.S. government

Fifth Infantry, *see* U.S. Army, Fifth Infantry

Flat, Tex., *see* Fort Griffin, Tex.

Flato, F. W., Jr., 82–83

Florida, 51

Floyd County, Tex., 2

Ford, Henry, 44

Ford County, Kan., 107–108

Ford County *Globe*, 110

Fort Clark, Tex., 14

Fort Concho, Tex., 43

Fort Dodge, Kan., 18

Fort Griffin, Tex., 90, 93–94; prosti-

tution in, 93–94

Fort Griffin *Echo*, 106

Fort Richardson, Tex., 17

Fort Sill, I.T., 4, 8, 21, 53

Fort Sully, D.T., 34

Fort Sumner, N.M., 5

Fort Worth, Tex., 65, 70, 82, 90, 101; meat-packing industry and, 90

Fort Worth *Democrat*, 90

Four Sixes (6666) Ranch, 13

Fourth Cavalry, *see* U.S. Army, Fourth Cavalry

Fowler, George, 85

Francklyn Land and Cattle Company, 2, 17, 22–23, 109, 127 (n. 6)

freighting, 16, 38, 63

Frio County, Tex., 65

Furgason, J. C., 84

gambling, 89, 91

Gamel, John W., 53

Gard, Wayne, 10

Garza, County, Tex., 119

George, M. B., 33–34

George Fowler, Son & Company, 85

George W. Saunders Commission Company, 70

Geronimo, Chief, 70

Gilman Reed & Company, 78

Glick, G. W., 108

Goliad, Tex., 3, 63, 67–68

Goliad County, Tex., 64

Gonzales, Tex., 81

Gonzales County, Tex., 67

Gooch, Ben, 16

Goodnight, Charles, 5–6, 11, 13, 106–107, 118, 148 (n. 27); career as transportation agent, 5–6

Goodnight-Loving Trail, 5, 43

Great Bend, Kan., 107

Great Plains, 18

Greer County, Tex., 22

Grimes County, Tex., 27

Groom, B. B., 22–23, 109

Guadalupe County, Tex., 30, 46, 71

Guide Map of the Texas Cattle Trail (pamphlet), 88

Hall, H. H., 70
Hannibal, Mo., 69
Hannibal and St. Joseph Railroad, 31–32, 74
Harris County, Tex., 28
Hashknife Ranch, 38
Hawlett, H. H., 108
Head, Richard G., 20, 37, 62
Hereford cattle, 65
Hidalgo County, Tex., 65
Hill, Ella, 95
Hill, Louis Hamilton, 95; *see also* Webb, Campbell, and Hill Land and Cattle Company
Hodges, Ben, 21–22
horse drives, 29–30, 48, 64, 68–70
House of Representatives, *see* U.S. Congress
Houston, Sam, 28
Hunter, J. Marvin, 11
Hunter, Janet (Webster), 78–79
Hunter, Robert D., 78–84, 111, 124, 148 (n. 27); career as commission agent, 80–84; career as meat packer, 82; career as transportation agent, 79–80
Hunter, Evans & Company, 81–83
Hyreson, George W., 98

ID (brand), 64
Idaho, 36
Idavale Ranch, 39
Iliff, John W., 37
Illinois, 31, 36, 73, 77–78, 80, 82–83, 85, 101, 106, 115; quarantine in, 106
Indiana, 60
Indians, 8, 17–18, 33–35, 37, 42–43, 50, 55, 60, 64, 88; cattle delivered to, 33–35, 37, 50; harassment of cattle drives by, 8, 17–18; *see also* specific tribes
Indian Territory, 3–4, 8, 35, 48, 50, 53, 57, 60, 65, 82–83, 107, 116; leasing of land in, 65, 82–83; quarantine (de facto) in, 48, 107
Iowa, 62
Ireland, 13
Ireland, John, 115

JA Ranch, 13
J. C. Furgason & Company, 84
J. L. Mitchener and Company, 77–78
J. T. Lytle & Company, 25
Jackman, William, 8
Jackson County, Tex., 66
Jacob Dold Company, 85
James Morrison Company, 85
James River Ranch, 24
Jennings, Joseph Pulliam, 46
Jennings, Susan (Crunk), 46
Jennings, William Henry, 25–26, 46; *see also* Blocker Brothers and Jennings Cattle Company
Johnson, W. W., 83
Johnson Coal Mining Company, 83
Jones, Jack, 54–55
Juan-Jinglero Company, Ltd., 20–21

Kansas, 2–5, 16–17, 20–21, 31–39, 42, 45–46, 48–49, 52–55, 60, 64–66, 71, 73–86, 88–89, 91–92, 96–97, 101, 103, 106, 108, 111–114, 117–118, 148 (n. 33); demands for quarantines in, 108; quarantines in, 92, 96–97, 107–108, 113–114, 117–118, 148 (n. 33)
Kansas City, Kan., 4, 33, 38, 73–78, 80–86, 89, 101; cattle trade and, 74–78, 80–86
Kansas City, Mo., 21
Kansas City Stock Yards Company, 74–86, 110; commission agencies and, 76–84; meat-packing industry and, 84–85; origin of, 74–75; volume of business of, 75
Kansas Pacific Railroad, 31–32, 74, 80, 88; number of cattle shipped by, 88
Karnes County, Tex., 61
Kaw River, 74–75, 85
Kerrville, Tex., 15, 17
King, Richard, 13
King Ranch, 13
Kingman & Company, Ltd. 85
Kinney County, Tex., 25
Kiowa Indians, 18
Knox County, Tex., 38

167

168

169